GROOMED FOR SUCCESS

GROOMED FOR SUCCESS

Johnny Richey

Copyright © 2021 by Johnny Richey.

All rights reserved. No part of this book may be reproduced in any form or by any electronic or mechanical means, including information storage and retrieval systems, without permission in writing from the publisher, except by reviewers, who may quote brief passages in a review.

ISBN: 978-1-956736-70-0 (Paperback Edition)
ISBN: 978-1-956736-71-7 (Hardcover Edition)
ISBN: 978-1-956736-69-4 (E-book Edition)

Some characters and events in this book are fictitious. Any similarity to the real persons, living or dead, is coincidental and not intended by the author.

Book Ordering Information

Phone Number: 315 288-7939 ext. 1000 or 347-901-4920
Email: info@globalsummithouse.com
Global Summit House
www.globalsummithouse.com

Printed in the United States of America

Contents

Foreword v

Lesson 1: Who Am I? 1

    Storms In My life 2
    Who Am I?
    Cause and Effect 6
    Who Am I?
    Getting to Know Your Demons (Negative Thoughts and
    Actions) 13
    Who Am I?|
    The Stranger Within 18
    Who Am I?
    Healing Power of the Mind 22
    Who Am I?
    Linking of the Soul and Spirit, Part 1 25
    What Do You Do When Stopped by Law Enforcement? ... 31

Lesson 2: Education and Transformation 40

    Education and Transformation 40
    Education and Transformation
    Rap music and Its Sedation 41
    Education and Transformation
    The Creation of Copycats 46
    Education and Transformation
    Gang Violence/At Risk Youth 60
    Education and Transformation
    Gangs Birthing Gangs 70
    Education and Transformation
    Why Gangs? 81

Education and Transformation
Moving the Mountain 107
What Do You Do When Stopped by Law
Enforcement, Part 2? 115

Lesson 3: Groomed For Success 117

Groomed for Success
Turning Boys into Men/ Girls into Ladies 118
Groomed for Success
Bridging the Gap 120
Groomed for Success
Linking of the Souls and Spirits, Part 2 123
Groomed for Success
Expression of Your Higher Self 125
The Expression of Your Inner/ Higher Self: 126
Bibliography 128

Dedication

This program is dedicated to all the parents who have lost their children to gang violence and at-risk behavior; to all the parents who have lost their children to any kind of violence; to children and youth who have lost their parents, other family members, and friends to gang violence. We hope that all of their souls are free now. This program was created as an answer to the solutions for gang violence, gang affiliation, and at risk behavior in our youth. Groomed for S will assist in transforming the youth mindsets and put them on healthy path toward successfully achieving their life's goals.

Foreword

Statistics show that juvenile crime is rising among youth ages 12-19, suicide rates are up compared to five years ago, and teen pregnancy among young girls ages 13-19 is also up. Drug addiction is on the rise among the youth of today and the dropout rate is alarming. The author of Groomed for Success' personal experience along with our daily observations and interactions with at risk youth and gang members have enabled us to create this self-discovery program for today's young people.

Groomed for Success understands that no child is born with an inherent nature to violence or deviant behavior. These are learned behaviors which stem from a host of societal factors. Some of these factors are negative media content, explicit lyrics in music, blood and gory graphics in video games, sexism in fashion, dramatization and sensationalism in news media and social networks, the internet, and a break down in the family structure. There is also a stigmatization towards urbanization. Rap artists are hailed as the prevailing heroes of our day to our youth and their provocative lyrics and imagery have become the lure by which young, impressionable minds gravitate towards.

There is a saying that "exposure = preference". Every culture is built on a foundation of beliefs. These beliefs shape the culture, the culture shape the people, and the people shape their lives. The powerful influence of the culture will affect factors such as values, communication, life style, worship, and so forth. When the core values in which a society is built on becomes weak, then the destruction of that society become imminent. By attacking the problem at its root we can eradicate the spread of this pernicious cancer.

Groomed for Success applies these methods and logic to the answer that targets the core problems of our youth today. Instead of ridiculing their misguided aspiration, we direct and channel them into discovering who they are and who they aspire to become. Through self-identification and self-discovery, we listen to and allow the youth to tell us what their issues are and how they will solve them. We attempt to peak their interests with what their desires and interests are. This identification and discovery program can be the catalyst that opens the door to free the youth from the clutches of gang and risky behaviors while transpiring the mind to operate in a healthy and positive manner. We understand that most youth today feel ostracized and cut off. They have adapted to an outlaw mentality and have become desensitized to the valves of life. Because of the broken condition of the family structure, the increases of drug and alcohol addicted parents, the environmental conditions of many inner city communities, and the rise of gangs across America, many of the youth of today are misguided and undereducated. They are left to themselves to fill a void of self-worth and belonging that they don't know how to fill. They turn to the streets and gangs and assimilate with the values of that culture. It is often too late that they find that many of their choices carries grave consequences such as jails, drug use and abuse, teen pregnancy, social stigmas, brutality, literacy, poverty, deprivation, and under education. This, in turn, becomes a centrifuge force that sucks them in. Groomed for Success takes an aggressive approach to curve this peril. The youth in our program will strive to be their very best in life. They will learn how to live a healthy and positive existence in a positive manner in society. They will be law abiding citizens with life and career goals.

Introduction

Groomed for Success introduces, educates, directs, and assists the young person in discovering the necessary methods and skills needed to eradicate the propensity of gang affiliation, gang violence, and at-risk behaviors in their lives. Groomed for Success is intensive and structured in semi study form with self-evaluating real life questions that engage the youth in critical thinking and decision making. Groomed for Success will reshape the participant's mode of thinking and give them self-awareness of their present situations. It will teach the young person how to positively respond to the stresses of peer pressure, gang affiliation, and at-risk behaviors.

Groomed for Success is an invaluable tool that will work with our young people in the juvenile justice system, the criminal justice system, and any other detention program that is seeking to address the crises facing our youth today. This program seeks to educate and transform young adults from all walks of life to become well rounded individuals with respect for the law, the men and women in uniform, and to become successful members of their society.

Because We Care

This program was created as a solution to address the problems of juvenile attitudes and violence toward one another and society. It is not just about the violence that the focus is being placed on, but rather what the underlying causes and issues are of the young person's mindset and subsequent actions.

Groomed for Success was created solely for the young person who is involved in a gang, have gang affiliations, and/or participates in at-risk behavior. It will assist them by looking at who they really are in all areas of their life. This is a self-discovery program in which the young adult what their issues are, discover the solutions to their issues, build a foundation based on their roadmap for success, and allow facilitators to assist them in being "Groomed for Success". Each lesson contains suggestions for workshops at the end with in-depth questions built to educate and transform the participants into well rounded citizens. The basis of Groomed for Success is that it is directed toward a path of discovery for the young adult. Getting to the core issues that plague our young people today requires only that they be guided to discover who they are and who they choose to become.

The Curriculum Format

Groomed for Success consists of nineteen lessons to account for the total program. Each lesson of the program is designed to adhere to specific issues in the young adult's life. In each lesson there are multiple steps that must be taken in order for the lessons to be complete.

Lesson 1 immediately begins to address the barriers and issues in the participant's life. The youth look at what their storms are (issues), how they (youth) played a part in their storms (problems), and what they could have done different. Lesson 1 also addresses childhood issues, soul searching, and different types of relationships.

In Lesson 1, there are seven components which are used to metamorphose and reshape youth behavior. The seven components are:
1) Storms in My Life
2) Cause and Effect
3) Getting to Know My Demons (negative thoughts)
4) The Stranger Within
5) The Healing Power of the Mind
6) Linking of the Soul and Spirit
7) What Do You Do When Stopped by Law Enforcement?
Each component is presented in a systematic logical fashion using standard procedures for cognitive behavioral intervention.

The seven components will teach the participant how to change their at-risk behaviors, how to think positive, social skills, self-refection, and uncovering antisocial thoughts. Groomed for Success will engage youth in pro-social interaction based on self-understanding and consideration of the impact of their actions on others. Groomed for Success integrates the seven components with an explicit step-by-step process for addressing the challenges and stressful real life situations in the young person's life.

>Lesson 1 - Opens the program with the overview of soul searching.
>Lesson 2 - The program focuses on education and transformation.
>Lesson 3 - Explores "Groomed for Success".

It provides a wrap up of the program with the option of extending the program based on the needs of the group members. For example, groups may opt to meet for additional sessions to learn new social skills that they have negotiated with their group facilitators along with further practice in applying cognitive self-change and problem solving skills to newly identified problem situations.

Lesson Format

Each lesson of Groomed for Success will end with a learning tool which will teach the participant how to respond when stopped by law enforcement. It will also teach them why it is important to obey and respect the law and the men and women in uniform.

Components of Lesson #1:

Who Am I?
1. Storms in My Life
2. Cause and Effect
3. Getting to Know Your Demons (negative thoughts)
4. Stranger Within
5. Healing Power of the Mind
6. Linking of the Soul and Spirit, 1
7. What Do You Do When Stopped by Law Enforcement?

After dealing with and resolving deep seeded issues and concerns in Lesson 1, the participant will have some measure of peace and will be ready to move on to Lesson 2, Education and Transformation.

Lesson 2 starts with Education and Transformation. In Lesson 2, facilitators will cover the influence of rap music in the lives of young people today, the beats, the sounds of gun shots in rap songs, the copycat syndrome, gang violence, gang affiliation, and at-risk behaviors. Lesson 2 ends with solutions that the participant themselves implement as viable solutions to their issues personally and as a whole. The participant ends Lesson 2 with having the solutions to gang violence and their own issues. The Components of Lesson #2 Education and Transformation:

1. Rap music and Its Sedation
2. Creation of Copycat
3. Gang violence and At-Risk Participant
4. Gangs Birthing Gangs
5. A Solution to Gang Violence
6. Moving the Mountain
7. What Do You Do When Stopped by Law Enforcement?

Groomed For Success

Lesson 3 is being "Groomed for Success". It is all about seeing the transformation in word and deed. In Lesson 3, the participant will utilize the skills they have acquired in Lessons 1 and 2. These are the skills which will allow participant to handle the stresses of life in a proper manner. They will have a solid Plan Of Production (POP) and a real life Roadmap For Success (RFS).

The Components of Lesson #3 Groomed for Success:

1. Turning Boys Into Men and Girls Into Women
2. Bridging the Gap
3. Linking of the Soul and Spirit, 2
4. The Expression of Your Higher Self
5. What Do You Do When Stopped by Law Enforcement?

Facilitator Guide for Lesson 1

The first workshop of Lesson 1 starts at the end of Session 3. It is a workshop that combines the material in the first three lessons and is designed for the participant to get in touch with themselves and to look over their lives mentally, spiritually, emotionally, and physically.

The second workshop in Lesson 1 is at the end of Session 5 entitled, "The Healing Power of the Mind". The participant will write out what they have learned and discovered about themselves.

The third workshop in Lesson 1 is at the end of Session 7, "What Do You Do When Stopped by Law Enforcement?" The participant will have the opportunity to interact with law enforcement to build respect for the men and women in uniform and to dismiss the myth that all law enforcement officers are bad. This will also teach participants in this program how to respect authority figures and give them the understanding that all law officers have a job to do just as any other working family member.

Facilitator Guide for Lesson 2

In Lesson 2, the participant will have the chance to see a transformation in self. This is where education and knowledge of self and building self respect starts. The curriculum in Lesson 2 reviews the participant's mindset in depth and allows them to bring out their issues related to being gang members, being gang affiliated, and/or exhibiting at-risk behaviors which have caused some influence to these negative behaviors.

Rap music and its sedation are main foresees. In Lesson 2, facilitators are observing the participant's transformation, how the participant is digesting the information, participant's mental comprehension of subjects, and how they are performing mentally, spiritually and physically. In Lesson 2, Session 1, the participant will tell facilitators how rap music has influenced them in any way, whether positive or negative. This technique will be executed from the participant's own thoughts and feelings. Facilitators and participants will also cover a few names of negative rap artists. Additionally in Lesson 2, participants will be completing intense profiles on themselves, roadmaps for their success (RMS), and plans of productions (POP). This workshop can be very helpful for participants' future goals and behavior modification.

The workshop will teach proper interaction with law enforcers at the end of Lesson 2. By this time, the participant will have a sense of ease and respect after knowing officers are just normal people with a job just like anyone else who work, pay taxes, who have loving families, pay bills, experience pains, troubles, and struggles in life, as we all have.

Facilitator Guide for Lesson 3

Turning boys into men and turning girls into women, Lesson 3, starts with fatherhood and motherhood. The participant will perform an evaluation on self and their broken relationships in Session 2 entitled, "Bridging the Gap". The facilitator will also conduct an evaluation on participant progress. During the last workshop, the participant will visit the community and the police station to have a sincere interaction with the men and women in uniform and be encouraged to join them in their academy, if possible.

Group Facilitator Selection

Groomed for Success recommends the ideal climate for group facilitation to include: empathy, facilitation/teaching techniques, understanding group processes, interpersonal interaction, and the ability to control a group of offenders, at-risk participants, or problem individuals through non-coercive means. We feel that this will be an emotional time for a portion of the group's members in Lesson 1. It is during Lesson 1 that the participant takes an intense look at themselves and their issues, the good, bad, and the ugly. Heavy emphasis is put on having a facilitator with a respectable and positive frame of mind and good techniques with participants to handle their emotional crises.

Group Member Selection

The group members (offenders, students, and at-risk participants) should be prescreened and selected after a brief individual interview. Such a meeting need not take any more than five to ten minutes. It should set the tone for the learning sessions, direct and focus the group member to the usefulness of the program in their own lives, and set expectations that positive participation would greatly enhance their options. This applies to all settings: prison, jail, or community.

Lessons/Sessions

For the purpose of this curriculum, lessons are defined as a unit of martial comprised activities and concepts which group members learn to apply to their daily life situations. This curriculum includes twenty-one lessons with the option of aftercare lessons left open. Sessions are defined as a unit of time in which groups meet to learn and practice the content taught in each lesson.

Sessions are usually one to two hours in duration but are a function of the agency or system implementing Groomed for Success and therefore may be longer in time. As such, it may take more than one session to complete all of the activities in a lesson.

Group facilitators should take care to deliver each lesson competently and efficiently but not hesitate to use a second session to complete its contents, if necessary.

Activity Introduction and Expectations

Prior to beginning Lesson 1, conduct a brief (5-10 minutes) interview with each of your group members.

The goals of the interview are to:
1. Lay the groundwork for reasonable expectations
2. Discuss ground rules (come to session ready to participate, have homework complete, and be ready to learn something new)
3. Build relationships by getting to know the group members (where he/she is from etc.)

Group Size/Frequency

While the size of the group may be determined by agency policy, it is recommended that groups include between twelve to eighteen members in order to preserve program integrity. More than eighteen group members, given the activities and learning involved with each lesson, would require more time than is allotted per group session. Fewer than twelve group members would compromise the group process and decrease the effectiveness of the group member's learning.

Most cognitive behavioral intervention is recommend at least two sessions per week. Groomed for Success' curriculum is best delivered two to three times per week. Facilitators are strongly encouraged to schedule a minimum of two sessions per week. The total number of the sessions per week is a function of staff resources, group members, and group facilitators, as well as policy direction from agency or jurisdiction executives.

Group Norms

The program should also have established group norms and expectations. While these may be based upon individual, institutional, or agency policy, the group norms should consider the learning environment and ensure the safety and security for all involved. As such, the group facilitator should consider the following as minimal group norms:

Confidentiality: It is expected that all information shared be kept within the group unless such information indicates possible harm to the individual or others. This norm is subjected to agency guidelines for disclosure (which should be shared with group members as applicable).

Respect what is shared: All statements should be accepted as learning information for learning purposes. Individuals should ensure that opinions and statements shared are constructive for the purpose of meeting the objective of the lesson and content of the curriculum.

Take turns speaking and sharing: Individuals need to speak one at a time, listen to what is being said, remain focused on the topic and subject matter, and provide opportunities for others to respond should they disagree with something.

No aggression or violence: Physical or verbal aggression and violence is not permitted and should not be tolerated.

Group facilitator preparation: Minimally, group facilitators should have attended formal facilitator trainings in Groomed for Success' curriculum before delivering the program.

While group facilitators have different styles and approaches to content delivery, all must know the content that must be delivered to group members.

Group facilitators should review each lesson and prepare its contents before each session. This includes practicing model displays until they are well rehearsed.

Have all material duplicated. Ensure that equipment work and that the physical plant is ready for the group to begin.

Ensure the room is well lit, ventilated, and arranged so that the chairs in a comfortable discussion type format (usually tables and chairs in a "U" shape format).

Finally, group facilitators have the option to extend the curriculum as described in lessons.

The decision to extend Groomed for Success after completion of the program may be based upon such factors as: length of stay of the group members within the agency or system, needs of individual group members, agency or system mandate, availability of staff, and fiscal resources.

As you facilitate groups using Groomed for Success' curriculum, keep in mind that the goal is to effect change in thinking so that behavior is positively impacted.

Good luck as you embark on a most challenging journey!

How to Implement the Lessons:

Lessons follow a similar format. Each lesson begins a story for the group facilitators to familiarize themselves with the summary and rationale of the lesson. Concepts and definitions are outlined with the learning objectives in the beginning of each lesson. Each lesson ends with questions which will engage group members into critical thinking and problem solving with an outline of the major learning tools in that lesson. The lesson is in a one column format, in which the content (the material that must be delivered to the group members) is at the beginning of the lesson for the group facilitator's directions.

JOHNNY RICHEY

Lesson 1

Who Am I?

Storms In My life

Ice Breaker:

Introduce yourself and your co-workers. Mention certain personal information about yourselves (such as your job or where you from). Introduce each member by name to the rest of the group (which city/town and state), not institution or facility.

Directions:

Participants will identify and address issues in their lives, past and present. They will discover solid solutions to their issues. Participants will also examine different kinds of relationships and feelings. Staff will observe participant participation, honesty, positive, and negative comment.

The participant looks at what their storms are, how they played a part in their storms, and what they could have done different. Participants will address childhood issues, perform soul searching, and examine different types of relationships. Facilitator would do well to anticipate that emotions will run high and negative behaviors will be acted out. Much attention, love, respect, and empathy must be presented and noted along with behaviors.

The Lesson:

Each of us, participant and adult alike, have gone through some type of storm in our lives. It is not so much about the storm that we go through as it is about the way we handle our storms and the outcomes. We have to approach each storm with confidence and a winning attitude.

In the past, you may have handled your storms in a negative way and the consequences or results usually were negative too. You may also have viewed your storms as a negative event in your life but many storms can be a valuable learning tool if observed in a different manner. You can learn many appreciated life lessons from going through storms; lessons that can be of help to yourself and others in the future. *Life lessons* are events in your life that you experience and learn from. The learning experience can be positive or negative. You get to choose. You oftentimes can control the outcome and it can be a winning and rewarding one if you handle the life event in a proper manner.

You need to always give your life events solid thought and think of the outcomes that you desire bearing in mind that it does not hurt or harm you or others in society. You must always be mindful and aware of your surroundings in society and know that you are a winner. Go about your day with a positive attitude.

Questions:
What are the life's storms that you have been through? Past and Present.

Give us 5 examples of *life lessons* that you have had to face.

Your Storms:

Not allowing your storms to overwhelm you and being prepared to meet your storms head on in a positive manner is what will enable you to become a winner. There are solutions to your issues and we will examine and address the issues for just what they are today. You must learn not to dwell on your problems and only on the solutions and being a winner in all aspects of your life. The ways to come up with the solutions to your issues is to examine yourself and find in *you* the root of your problems. You must get to the core and go from there. A lot of instances will occur when you begin to dig deep within yourself that things will get tough and it is at these times that you must dig deeper. As the old saying goes, "You must go through it, to get to it".

Questions:
What is *it* in itself? What is *its* nature? What is the inside or outside influence?

Life's Issues

Taking a long hard look at your issues and taking them one day at a time is the first step to learning how to implement new and betters skills to solve your life issues. You must remain strong and persevere. We all know or have heard of people who have committed suicide, killed others, and turned to drugs, alcohol, and pills. They chose not to go through their storm. You need to know your own view of the world in which you live and your immediate community. You must see the world through your own eyes and not the eyes of others. One way to look at your issues is to look at what role you played in each issue.

Questions:
Why did it occur?
Could you have stopped it from occurring?
What did you do or say? Positive or Negative.
What were your immediate actions? Positive or Negative.
What could you have done differently?
How do you feel about it now?

Relationships:

Building positive and strong relationships with yourself, family, community, and peers is another key task that you have to work on and in some cases, work through to be successful. It takes hard work and dedication to build and maintain relationships of all types whether they are personal or professional. Relationships are important to have in the world and we should keep our attention focused on positive and healthy relationships. You also have to keep your relationships authentic and truthful. Remember that you must keep a positive and healthy relationship with yourself also.

Questions:
What type of relationships do you have with others?
How do you view your relationships with the following?
How would you like your relationships to be with the following?
Self?
Family?
Peer?
Society? Law Enforcement? Spiritual leadership?
Community? Professional?

Who Am I?

Cause and Effect

Directions:

Participant will examine the cause and effect of their behavior, gang violence, gang affiliation, and at-risk behavior. Participant then will create solutions to counteract the negative behavior.

Lesson:

Young adults live out in their lives by what they learn from others, their parents, guardians, siblings, relatives, peers, and main stream media. Here we will look into the causes and effects of the underlying issues that young people are facing today and some of the past issues that are still having a negative effect in their lives. Participants must be honest with self about what their real issues are and find the causes of them. Path of self-discovery is a process that will lead the participant to the beginning of getting at their core issues. Once they know the causes of their issues then they can begin to start to go about the business of solving their issues one by one.

Most of our core issues and causes stem from birth to five years of age. We will look at the different stages of the participant's issues of causes in their life and at what age they occurred.

Questions:

What can you remember from childhood and what age were you? Positive or Negative.

Have you had any life changing events happen in your life from age 0-5 years? 6-13 years?

Do you think that any of your behaviors today are directly related to or derived from causes of events that you experienced from 0-5 years of age? 6-13 years of age?

Can you be honest about your feelings and the causes of issues in your life?

Do you want to be free of these issues?

Affected By Life:

All events in the participant's life, whether they are negative or positive, have an effect on them and most times, society and others. Many of the effects that derive from their actions are not of their own circumstances but the situations that they grew up in. A portion of the participants are raised in what society considers "good homes", while others are said to have been raised in "bad homes". "Good homes" are homes where there were two parents in the home and the children were taught to love, respect, and honor one another. Those parents instilled character in their children and they were taught morals, principles, and values to become well-rounded individuals.

"Bad homes" are homes where the children may or may not have had two parents in the home, parents had little or no education, had low income, and where there is an absence of proper parenting skills. A lot of neglect and abuse are present in these homes.

It does matter that the participant came from a "good home" or a "bad home" because in examining their home life they will find the core effects that their upbringing had on them. It matters that the participant addresses the causes and effects that their home life has had and may still be having on them. We will now examine the effects that their home life had on them. It is time for some self-discovery.

Questions:

Which type of home were you raised in? "Good home"? "Bad home"?

How did you feel about your home life?

Were you happy in your home?

Do you think your parents/guardians did a good job in raising you?

How do you feel about your parents/guardians?

Was there neglect in the home? Abuse?

How did you get along with others in the home?

Was there drinking and drug abuse in the home? Social drinking?

What were you taught about law enforcement?

Were there any spiritual or religious practices in the home?

Were holidays celebrated and how?

Were your parents able to provide for your needs? Wants?

Was school mandatory or not?

Were you taught about education and finances?

Did your family sit down and dine together in the home? Why? Why not?

Why Gangs?

There are many different reasons why the youth of today are affiliated with gangs and are displaying at-risk behavior. We will look at some of the reasons. We will also take a closer look at the causes and effects of being in a gang, affiliation with gangs, and exhibiting at-risk behavior. Many of us know people who fit into all three of these categories and maybe the participant fits into one or more of these categories.

Peer pressure: This is pressure that is influenced over another to get that individual to conform to the group's norm. Be a successful leader!

Low self-esteem: Low self-esteem is a sense of not feeling good about yourself and what you think others might feel or think about you. You are beautiful and you're one of a kind!

People: People come into your lives and not always for the good. Everyone knows people whom they wish they had never met. You have to be very selective about who you allow to be a part of your success. Not everyone is going to be happy for you and some may want to hold on and not let go. You must make peace and break free from your past!

Places: Clubs, parties, learning institutions, the streets, and certain homes are often places where drugs, alcohol, neglect, abuse, and bad behavior is prevalent. You have the power within yourself to rise above any and all circumstances!

Drugs: It is a fact that most young adults are using some form of drugs and alcohol. Drugs are a dead end all the way around. Nothing good will ever come out of the use of drugs. Say no to drugs and stay away from drugs and those who use and sell drugs Winners do not use drugs!

Family Initiations: Sometimes there are family members who are in and affiliated with gangs who may also exercise negative behavior in the presence of the participant. It does not matter who it is or what the situation may be, you should always choose to do the right thing!

Friends: Everyone who you say is your friend is not your friend. Friendships are built over time and require a lot of love, respect, and honesty. Friends will tell you the truth even when you don't want to hear it and they won't tell you anything that will put you in harm's way or get you in trouble. You have it in you to build lasting and loving relationships with family and friends!

Environmental Conditions: A lot of times your environment can define who you become. It does not matter if the conditions in which you grew up were negative or positive, only you can define and become the person that you want to be!

Violence: Many of you have experienced violence in and out of the home in some form. Violence is never the answer. You are able to communicate your feelings in a positive manner!

Feelings of not being loved: Some of you today are experiencing depression and anxiety because you may feel that you are not loved. Those feelings then take the form of an action and you begin to act out.

Questions:
Have you ever felt that no one loves or cares for you, and if so, why?

Do you still feel that way?

What are some ways that you have acted out when you didn't feel loved or felt neglected?

Here are a few exercises for the participant that will get their minds to thinking about their future.

Challenges: You must meet the challenges of everyday life in a positive and healthy way. This is how you will come to understand and learn to be successful in your life. Overcoming your challenges will empower you to be and do your best in all areas of your life!

What do you see as any challenges in your life at this present time

Meeting goals: You must meet your goals in life with small steps at first but you must also meet them with determination.

Write out five goals that you want to accomplish in the next five years in order of importance.

Courage: Take the time and patience to be who you want to be from the knowledge you have learned from others' mistakes and successes, study hard in school, and do your homework. Go that exact mile.

What is your definition of courage?

Confidence: Know that nothing comes to you without hard work. Know that you should also place positive people around who will support you as you support others. Their positive feedback will give you confidence, knowing you're on the right path.

On a scale of 1-10 how would you rate your confidence level and why?

Production: As you become successful in life, see yourself in a career, attend a great college and own your own business, you can know without doubt that your life is headed in a positive direction.

It is a known fact that whatever it is that you are willing to put into your future and your career is what you will get out. You have to be productive to become successful!

Are you ready to develop your personal plan of production?

Now we will develop solutions to counteract at-risk behaviors that the young person has displayed in the past. This exercise will require facilitator and student's interaction.

"Be the winner in your life…Be Groomed for Success"

Write down several solutions that you think will help you to turn your behaviors around. Be true to yourself!

Who Am I?

Getting to Know Your Demons (Negative Thoughts and Actions)

Directions:

Participant will identify what they consider to be their demons and implement behaviors that will free them from their stresses and anxieties.

Lesson:

How well do you know yourself? How well do you think that you know what makes you react to things and people? If you feel that you are in a battle at this time then who would that battle be with emotionally, mentally, and spiritually? Do you think that you are controlled by any people or events outside of yourself, and if so, in what way?

In getting to know your demons (any negative thing or event that impedes you or causes havoc and /or harm in your life), it is essential that you take a honest, hard look at yourself in at least four areas of your life; mentally, spiritually, emotionally, and physically. When you examine yourself in these four areas of your life, you will then start to better understand who you are and what makes you act. You have to know who you are to mature into becoming who you want to be. You model the individual that you want to be. You have to choose.

Everyone experiences demons, evil thoughts of revenge, heart aches, emotional setbacks, hurt feelings, betrayal, cheated on, character assassination, hatred, jealousy, envy, coveting, and many others. It is whatever hinders you. You must identify and address these issues so that you will be free to move on to a better life. This will be a life that you will tailor just for you.

Spiritually, it is a good thing to believe in something or someone higher than yourselves, and yes, you must choose. You can't live by what you think spirituality means to others, but only by what it means for you and what your understanding and expression is. Spirituality is a connection with a higher being and you have to determine what that higher being means to you. It is not necessarily religion.

Questions:
Do you think you are a spiritual person and why?

What does spirituality mean to you?

Stabilizing Emotions:

Emotionally, you have to become stable and capable of controlling yourself at all times and in all situations. Many actions arrive out of emotions which is why it is imperative that you learn to keep your whole person together no matter what. This is where you investigate what sets your emotions off and why.

Make a list of the things, people, or events that have or could set your emotions off in a negative way.

1   6
2   7
3   8
4   9
5   10

Mentally, you must come to a state of mind which allows you to make responsible and productive decisions for your life. You must honestly examine your past, decide what type of future you would like to have, and go about your business to get the job done to become successful, whatever that entails for you.

Questions:
How do you view your state of mind right now?
Do you think that you are responsible?
Do you make good decisions?
What does your past look like?
What does your future look like?
What will you do to be successful in your life?

Physically, you need to have a regime that consists of a proper diet and exercise. You must commit to taking care of your body thus assuring yourself longevity in life. Having a proper diet and exercise in your life gives you more drive.

Questions:
Do you eat healthy? Why or why not?
Do you exercise? Why or why not?
Do you want to take better care of yourself?

Plan of Production:

What exactly will you do to achieve the changes that you want to implement into your life?

Spiritually

Emotionally

Mentally

Workshop 1

This workshop will entail a discovery of "Storms In My life", "Causes and Effects", and "Getting to Know My Demons".

Participants are required to write a paper summarizing their storms, their causes and effects, and what their demons are (negative thoughts and actions).

Participant will also include in this paper what they feel will be their best solution in addressing their storms, causes and effects, and their demons.

In writing this paper, participant will be exercising self-discovery skills as well as getting to know their true self. Participants should remember that being totally honest while writing this paper will give them a good look at who they are and who they will strive to become. This information will be added to participants' POP (Plan of Production) and will begin their RTS (Roadmap to Success).

Who Am I?

The Stranger Within

Directions:

This is where participants discover who they are and which direction they want to take in life. Participants will perform a full self-examination that will act as a sort of roadmap for future progress and success in the program.

Lesson:

Who is the stranger within you? Do you know? Would you like to find out? It may not be a pretty sight but you have the ability within yourself to change who you are. You may hear many people tell you that you can become whoever it is that you want to become but when you look around and observe your environment and your immediate situation, you may think that the only options open to you are what you observe in your immediate environment and community. Do not be mistaken. You can change your life around the very moment that you decide you want change. Only you can make the necessary changes needed in your life. Others may assist you in your change but the initial decision to change, the necessary commitment, and the work put forward, must be all you.

Write a paragraph or two about who you are or who you think you are.

The Perception of Youth:

Let's examine what you look like to yourself and how you think about yourself. We will also look at how others in society look at you and why.

Many in our society are afraid of young adults today and because so, they don't hold a very high opinion of them. It is a fact that not all young people are bad or even exhibit negative behavior but that doesn't stop society from labeling and stereotyping you. Once you come to know who you are and how life and the world in which you live in really works, then you will find yourselves proud members of a generation of young people who work towards changing society's opinion about them. You will do this by being a leader and living a positive life, helping out in your community, and maybe even changing a few lives for the better. You have all of this power within you, you just have to learn how to exercise it.

Before you can go out into your community and city to do what is right and just, you must learn who you are and what it is you want to do. You must always have a plan and each day you must get up and be about your business in exercising your life's plan. Life is fun and can be very rewarding but it is also *your* business.

Write a paragraph about how you think the community and others view you.

Natural Law (Law of Nature)

Natural law or the law of nature is a universal law that is determined by nature. Natural law is a view that certain rights or values are inherent in or universally cognizable by virtue of human reason or human nature. Some people believe that there are laws which govern our inner being. They feel that when a person engages in a negative action it is said to have been an action that worked against the law of nature. You will know this to be true for yourself because many of you may have already experienced this event. You do something, you feel bad about it, and you wish you could reverse the situation but you cannot. You may be able to rectify some situations, but not all. The law of nature explains that you are a being who automatically thinks to do the right thing in your life. We cannot blame anyone for our short comings but self. You, yourself, possess all the positive energy needed to be successful in your life. There is only one power that you need to focus on and that is the power of positive energy. Nothing and no one has power over you unless you choose to relinquish it. You have the ability to resist. Do not give your power away!

To give your power to any person, place, or thing means that you are surrendering your own "free will". Free will is what you exercise when you make any decision in life, rather it is choosing what time you will awake in the morning or deciding whether to attend college. Oftentimes, there are many outside influences that have a lot to do with the way you exercise your free will but when it comes down to it, (the truth) you choose for your own life.

All that you need lies inside of you. You just have to bring it out and begin to exercise it. If you decide to waste your time and energy with negative people then you will receive negative responses in turn but if you choose to invest your time and energy in positive people and by doing positive things, you will in turn receive positive responses and results.

Questions:

What is your definition of cognizable and natural law (law of nature)?

What would you say are your shortcomings?

What power of positive energy do you possess?

How will you use your power? What outside influences have you given your power over to?

Which actions will you take to stop wasting your time and energy and giving your power away?

Who Am I?

Healing Power of the Mind

Directions:

We will now examine the power of the mind and its ability to assist with therapies that participants need to begin their transformation. They will come to understand just how important it is to think in a positive manner, to be attentive to their needs, the needs of their community, and environment. Participants will discover the power that is within them.

Lesson:

In looking at how your mind functions and why it is important to explore and have some kind of understanding of your mindset and mental capacities, you learn to think before making decisions and you learn also how to weigh your options. The mind is the set of cognitive faculties that enables consciousness, perception, thinking, judgment, and memory- a characteristic of humans.

Whatever its relation to the physical body, it is generally agreed that mind is that which enables a being to have subjective awareness and intentionality towards their environment, to perceive and respond to stimuli with some kind of agency, and to have consciousness, including thinking and feeling.

It is important to maintain a mindset that gravitates towards the core fundamental values that you learned about in the previous section. This mindset will be what you exercise when dealing with yourself and others. It says that you are aware and your intentions towards self and others are pure and without any kind of malice, that you understand and knowingly respond to self and others in a healthy and positive manner, that there is a certain amount of thought and feeling that goes into all of your interactions with self and others, and that you operate out of positive energy.

It is equally important to be aware and conscious of your body, its needs and wants. Eating a proper diet and incorporating a weekly exercise regime is essential to maintaining a healthy body. This regime will be of major benefit in your future and aids in the building of positive routines in your life.

You must remember that it is "you" who owns your mind and body and it will be up to you to maintain both mind and body. When others are vulnerable, your light at that time will appear on the scene and shine. Your positive conscious will go to work and work together awakening spirits and souls which lay dormant and struggle to believe again in righteousness and truth.

You are that light and that consciousness which will appear on the scene. Your positive energy, which you already possess inside of yourself, is now ready for you to access. It will put you on your path to be "Groomed for Success". You can be re-birthed in your mind and body and be completely in control. This is being designed specifically for you by you. You possess the solution. You are a winner!

You are all here on earth for a reason. You have many different talents, some hidden and some not. You are all gifted with something that you can do which no one else can do quite like you or as well as you. You are allowed to use your mind and body to benefit you in any resourceful, healthy, and positive manner that you can.

Questions:

Write out a weekly exercise regime for yourself.

Workshop 2

This workshop will require the participant to write a summary of each section. In this summary, participants will tell what they have learned from each lesson, and how it helped them, and what they discovered.

Law Enforcement Workshop

This workshop will consist of participants expressing their feelings about the men and women in uniform.

Officers of the law will be speaking, when possible.

Who Am I?

Linking of the Soul and Spirit, Part 1

Directions:

We will now examine and discuss the fundamentals of mutual respect, mutual love for mankind, and self-love. This is a very important part of the student becoming "Groomed for Success". Participants will be observing the linking of their conscious mind to respect, self-love, and humanity. The linking of the souls will direct them on the path to being compassionate to others, forgiving those in their past, and understanding others' short-comings, sufferings, happiness, and joys. They will observe and address these fundamentals in their life, other people lives, and society as a whole.

What exactly are the fundamentals of mutual respect and love? Let's find out.

"Love is a variety of different feelings, states, and attitudes that ranges from interpersonal affection ("I love my mother") to pleasure ("I loved that meal"). It can refer to an emotion of a strong and personal attachment. It can also be a virtue representing human kindness, compassion, and affection, "the unselfish loyal and benevolent concern for the good of another". It may also describe compassionate and affectionate actions towards other humans, one's self, or animals.

Respect is a positive feeling of esteem or deference for a person or other entity (such as nation or a religion), and also specific actions and conduct representative of that esteem. Respect can be a specific feeling of regard for the actual qualities of the one respected (I have great respect for her judgment). It can also be conduct in accord with a specific ethic of respect. Rude conduct is usually considered to indicate a lack of respect."

"Self-love is the love of oneself. Psychologist and social philosopher, Erich Fromm proposed that loving oneself is different from being arrogant, conceited, or egocentric. He proposed that loving oneself means caring about oneself, taking responsibility for oneself, respecting oneself, and knowing oneself (e.g. being realistic and honest about one's strengths and weaknesses). He proposed further, that in order to be able to truly love another person, a person needs first to love oneself in this way."

The importance of possessing self-love, respect, and love for others is that it helps to build character, integrity, and dignity. These qualities are necessary to interact and maintain healthy relationships.

The spirit and soul of the human race adhere to one another. This is found especially true in family members and friends. There is a union which comes from and is experienced through your interactions with other people. Psychic impressions of suffering emotions or some kind of traumatic experiences which have happened to a loved one is something you can feel. Your psychic or spirit can sense when something happens to your loved ones. We share the experiences of those souls and spirits of those present and from others whose lives have passed.

Bad experiences from the past, which some of you grew up in, have caused you to be desensitized from your living conditions which also have brought you to your present mindsets. These events have not allowed your spirit and soul to connect and feel the negative or positive impressions of others. You have relinquished your self-love, self-respect, and love for other because of many negative circumstances that you have endured in your life. You *are not* a product of your environment and you possess the ability to rise above your circumstances.

Some of you may be buried under emotional debris but when you look deep within yourselves, with honesty and truth, you will find that love for self and the respect and love for others is still inside of you. You have only to discover your true selves and release the brilliance that you have inside of you to begin your positive transition.

Exercising compassion for self and others allow you to connect with yourself and others on a spiritual, emotional, and mental level which is symbolic of normal everyday human interaction. You start to understand the feelings of others by expressing your own compassion for self and others. Understanding what you need in your life and what others require of you will give you the essential insight into the knowledge of life and self. Wisdom comes with understanding and good decision making.

Forgiveness frees you up to become the person you want to be. You cannot live a healthy existence holding on to old hurts and pains. In life, you will experience ups and downs, hurts and pains, and other sorrows but you must deal with these issues with understanding and compassion, always exercising forgiveness, compassion, and love. Exercising the fundamentals of self-love, respect, compassion, and forgiveness are processes that you will need to be familiar in order to be successful in life.

Questions:

Do you think that you have been desensitized to the above fundamentals?

What are some of your life experiences where you have had to exercise any of the fundamentals listed above?

What were the outcomes?

Which of these fundamentals or lack thereof do you think directly contributed to the mindset that you possess now?

What do you propose to do to change this mindset?

How has society and social media affected you concerning these fundamentals?

How has your immediate surroundings, family, living conditions, church, and community affected these fundamentals?

What is your own perspective about these fundamentals?

What is it that you would like to change about your view and experiences with these fundamentals?

Workshop 2

In this workshop, participants will conduct more self-discovery exercises. All information in this workshop is to be included in their POP.

This is a two part paper. It will be based on all the questions the participant answered in "The Stranger Within", "The Healing Powers of the Mind", and "Linking of the Soul and Spirit".

In Part 1, participants are to put together a picture of who they are. The information for this paper will come from each question that they answered in the previous three sections. Participants should be in-depth with their answers for most of the questions that they answer. This paper should be in essay form. Participants must have a staff member review Part 1 of their paper before proceeding to Part 2.

In Part 2, participants, using the same paper, will examine it, and select the things that they want to change and highlight them. Participants must meet with staff members after they highlight Part 1.

Participants will then rewrite the paper, causing it to reflect the person whom they are grooming themselves to be. Participants must keep both papers. This will be an intense paper. Participant must discover how they are going to implement the changes that are needed to be made in their life.

Karma:

Now let's take a look at what we call "Karma". Karma is the principle of *causality* where intent and actions of an individual influence for the future of that individual. Good intent and good deed contribute to good "karma" and future happiness, while bad intent and bad deed contribute to bad "karma" and future suffering.

What is your definition of karma?

Not everyone believes in karma and that is okay because you must respect others' beliefs and disbeliefs but if you do believe in karma then you have to believe that you will not be able to go about your business everyday doing wrong and hurting others assuming that good things will happen to you because it won't.

Assignment:

Now participant will begin a new discovery in a very different approach. Using all of the questions and paragraphs that they have already answered in this section and the questions below, participant will create their own self-assessment.

Name:

How would you like others to address you?

Write a summary of your life to include the following, but not limited to:

Your pros and cons.

Your beliefs and/or disbeliefs.

Your strengths and weaknesses.

Your favorite color or colors.

Who you love.

Who you trust.

Who you rely on.

Who relies on you.

How the world looks to you.

What is your "Higher Power" if you have one?

Do you have any goals?

What are your goals in life?

Where do you see yourself in nine months from now? Eighteen months? Three years?

This self-assessment should be at least five pages in length and you must give depth to your responses. These responses should be written in essay form and help will be provided. This self-assessment will be for your use only so it is recommended that you be very specific and honest. "To thy own self be true".

What Do You Do When Stopped by Law Enforcement?

Groomed for Success:

During this informative work shop, you will learn and be prepared for what to do when stopped and/or if you have an encounter with law enforcement. You will also have the opportunity at the end of this work shop to interact and build respect for the law and the men and women in uniform.

This work shop is entitled, "What Do You Do When Stopped by Law Enforcement".

Lesson:

An officer of the law has a job to do just as any other person who works. It is their job to protect and serve. You must understand that officers of the law are people just like you. They have families and loved ones as you and me. Seeing law officers from their point of view is something you may want to consider in revamping your attitude towards them.

The young people today must know how to address Law Enforcement when they are being stopped for any reason. Many of our young adults have a very negative perception of law enforcement officers. Some of these perceptions are from your own personal experiences and the experiences of others in your community, as well as what you may have seen on television. Many of you have a rude and disrespectful attitude towards law officers. This rude and disrespectful demeanor only escalates the situation. At some time in your life, you, more than likely, will encounter some type of interaction with Law Enforcement and will need to exercise yourself in a proper manner. Addressing law enforcement when facing a stop or a traffic violation with meekness and not a negative attitude toward Law Enforcement, may extend your life.

There are five fundamental responsive techniques that you will always use when stopped or having an encounter with Law Enforcement. They are respect, attitude, precautions, reaction to commands, and accountability. These virtues will be a major benefit to you in building your relationship with the men and women in uniform. If you are in a car driving, walking by yourself, in a group, in a home where there is domestic violence, at a gathering with friends in your home, at a party, or at family functions, if Law Enforcement comes to your home, residence, or your car, no weapon should be in your hands, laying next to you, or visible, even if you do have a license or permit for that weapon. Your immediate reaction when you have an encounter with law officers should always be mindful of the following:

1 Respect
2 Your attitude
3 Your precautions
4 Your reaction to commands
5 Your accountability

First-be respectful

Be respectful at all times. This means when law enforcement officers ask you for your license, registration, and insurance, your response should be, "Yes, Sir", or "Yes, Ma'am, here it is."

How do you respect a law enforcer if stopped by one? You show humility, kindness, and concern about why you are being stopped.

Attitude:

Obey all commands. How do you obey all commands? You are to do all that is asked of you by the law enforcer. What can happen if you do not obey all of the law enforcer's commands? Law enforcers can use force and take you to jail. They can even use deadly force if you are not cooperating with their commands.

Precaution:

Move slowly unless officers ask you to move differently. You should move slowly and reach for nothing unless you are instructed to do so by the law enforcers. Your hands should be on the steering wheel in plain sight when stopped by law enforcement or placed where the law enforcers can see your hands clearly. Why should you move slowly? Moving too fast can make law enforcers nervous or suspicious of you if you are reacting too fast or inappropriately.

Reaction to commands:

You must cooperate to all that is asked of you. Why should you cooperate to all commands that are asked of you? Because law enforcers lives are and can be in jeopardy when they are making traffic stops and so can your life too at any given time in or during a traffic stop. For this reason, your full cooperation and mannerism is needed at that time which will help you to a great extent.

Accountability:

When stopped by law enforcers, do not show any rage, anger, or aggression. Your attitude at that time during a traffic stop will be monitored along with your mannerism and body gestures. Remember, Law enforcers are only people with a job and like anyone else, could have had a bad day. Your responsibility is to cooperate with law enforcement at that time or during a traffic stop and allow the results of that encounter to end as quickly as possible with a positive outcome.

Why should you follow these instructions? Following these five instructions will save lives if implemented. The first thing you do is show respect and obedience. Second, obey all commands. Don't reach for anything unless you are asked by the officers and that is what the officer wants to see. Thirdly, move slowly unless asked to move differently. If the officers ask you to get on the ground, you get on the ground as fast as possible. Don't give the officers a reason to fire a taser weapon at you or shoot you. Number four, cooperate with all that is asked of you by the officers and never volunteer any information unless you are asked. Be truthful and do not lie about the information you give and always show concern about the questions with respect and cooperation. Five, do not show any rage, hate, anger, aggression, or disrespect toward any law enforcement officers, male or female while in uniform.

What do you do when stopped by law enforcement? Do whatever it takes to stay out of harm's way.

What are your rights when stopped by law enforcement?

You have your Miranda rights. After giving law enforcement officers your license, insurance, and registration, you have rights.

The Miranda Warning states:

"You have the right to remain silent. Anything you say can and will be used against you in a court of law. You have the right to an attorney. If you cannot afford an attorney, one will be provided for you. Do you understand the rights I have just read to you?"

The warning, which is intended to inform you of your rights regarding police questioning, does not have to be read to you if you are not placed under arrest. The reason for this is that if you are not arrested for committing a crime, you are not going to trial so you don't need to be warned that what you say can be used against you during trial. However, if the officer does conduct pre-arrest questioning and feels that the suspect is beginning to make self-incriminating statements, the officer will read the Miranda Warning in order to protect the suspect's rights and to ensure the statements may be used in court.

You cannot be arrested for simply refusing to answer the officer's questions however, police can arrest you for other reasons such as probable cause. It is important to be polite and avoid aggravating the situation. Refusing to answer questions before being arrested may look suspicious and can be mentioned during trial. Therefore, if you wish to remain silent you should say that your attorney advised you not to answer any questions without him or her present.

You can be arrested without being read your Miranda Rights. The Miranda rights do not protect you from being arrested, only from incriminating yourself during questioning. All police need to legally arrest a person is "probable cause" -- an adequate reason based on facts and events to believe the person has committed a crime.

Police are required to "Read him his (Miranda) rights," only before interrogating a suspect. While failure to do so may cause any subsequent statements to be thrown out of court, the arrest may still be legal and valid.

Also without reading the Miranda rights, police are allowed to ask routine questions like name, address, date of birth, and Social Security number necessary to establishing a person's identity. Police can also administer alcohol and drug tests without warning, but persons being tested may refuse to answer questions during the tests.

1. You have the right to remain silent.

The Court: "At the outset, if a person in custody is to be subjected to interrogation, he must first be informed in clear and unequivocal terms that he has the right to remain silent."

2. Anything you say can be used against you in a court of law.

The Court: "The warning of the right to remain silent must be accompanied by the explanation that anything said can and will be used against the individual in court."

3. You have the right to have an attorney present now and during any future questioning.

The Court: "...the right to have counsel present at the interrogation is indispensable to the protection of the Fifth Amendment privilege under the system we delineate today. ... [Accordingly] we hold that an individual held for interrogation must be clearly informed that he has the right to consult with a lawyer and to have the lawyer with him during interrogation under the system for protecting the privilege we delineate today."

4. If you cannot afford an attorney, one will be appointed to you free of charge if you wish.

Cognitive Interviewing Investigative Statement Analysis

The Court: "In order fully to apprise a person interrogated of the extent of his rights under this system then, it is necessary to warn him not only that he has the right to consult with an attorney, but also that if he is indigent a lawyer will be appointed to represent him. Without this additional warning, the admonition of the right to consult with counsel would often be understood as meaning only that he can consult with a lawyer if he has one or has the funds to obtain one.

The Court continues by declaring what the police must do if the person being interrogated indicates that he or she does want a lawyer...

"If the individual states that he wants an attorney, the interrogation must cease until an attorney is present. At that time, the individual must have an opportunity to confer with the attorney and to have him present during any subsequent questioning. If the individual cannot obtain an attorney and he indicates that he wants one before speaking to police, they must respect his decision to remain silent."

Active Behavioral Conduct:

1. Remember to think before speaking.
2. Remember to think before doing.
3. Remember to give the other person the benefit of the doubt, especially when strong feelings are involved.
4. Remember, given the same situation and/or circumstances, you could have been viewed as that same selfish and unreasonable person who confronted you unfairly.

5. Remember to look for fact and truth of the matter.
6. Remember to try and win the person not the argument.
7. Remember that all things have at least two sides but no one has enough wisdom to see them all.
8. Remember that respect precludes prejudices of all kinds toward others and wards off vexation of spirit, mind, and body.
9. Remember there are realities of your life which will become more valuable with age.
10. Remember that there are only two entities that are fundamental to reality: they are communication and transportation (influence and motivation).
11. Remember that reality must be equal.
12. Remember that your life has only the value you place on it at any given time.
13. Remember that money does not buy truths.
14. Remember that no person or thing planned their time or place to be born are created.
15. Remember that the most any person can be responsible for is giving others their best effort, if it is truly their best effort.
16. Remember that alliance forces have no favorites; it provides a living environment for all from the amoeba to humans.
17. Remember that each living being instinctively knows its needs but has no control over the forces that provides them, each one dependent on the other.
18. Remember that compassion is a human asset if used unselfishly, but a liability otherwise.
19. Remember that miscommunication is far worse than no communication.
20. Remember that consistency is the key to success in many relationships.
21. Remember that each of us has a purpose and a small part of that purpose is to know what that purpose is, the rest is performance.

22. The wisdom of opportunity is preparation. Opportunity will only benefit those who are prepared to perform.

The Protocol of a Positive Mind:

Selecting: The right decisions and choices, all things depend upon the wisdom to make the right decision and choice at the right time.

Selections: Choices or acts upon who, what, where, when, how, and why.

Preparation: Success is always affected by how well a person is prepared to perform the task at hand.

Dictation: Success is equally affected by the amount of dictation, determination, and passion connected from the person to the task at hand.

Follow through success is finally backing up by following through and completing the task at hand in standard life.

Standardization: Ongoing success is affected by whether a person standardizes him or her performance so they can be repeated with the same results over and over again, the mark of the winner and especially a champion.

Make yourself an achiever and from those goals you will become who you are.

Lesson 2

Education and Transformation

Education and Transformation

Rap music and Its Sedation

Directions:

Participant will now examine rap music, its lyrics, and beats. They will also examine the influence of rap music in their life and society and what kind of stimulation rap music has had on the participant. Participant will look at whether rap music has had a positive or negative impact in their life.

Lesson:

You have heard guns blasting in rap music and many messages of violence embedded in the lyrics of it. Many of the young people today listen to rap music. Some of them are going wild over the beats and lyrics contained in rap music. Are you persuaded by the music to live an illusion?
Using marijuana, ecstasy, alcoholic beverages, and other hallucinogenic drugs only causes false character, negative personality changes, and a slow or fast ride to nowhere. Rap music, mixed with drugs and alcohol, is a very bad mix, especially if you are a person who is easily influenced.
Many young adults today imitate rappers and glorify the gangster styled rap music. They have not fully understood that the majority of the artists who rap about the gangster lifestyle don't live that way themselves. Many of the young people have issues already and couple those issues with gangster rap music, drugs, and alcohol, their mind starts to engage in delusions and hallucinations causing them to make terrible choices. This gangster rap music gives young people make believe ideas of quick money, pretty women, fine jewelry, fancy cars, and million-dollar homes.

Do you believe that negative desires can be aroused by listening to negative rap music? If so, why and how?

In rap music, with its provocative videos which stimulates the conscious and the unconscious mind, the lyrics, instrumental beats, and video images are implanted in the subconscious mind. These images and lyrics take root and begin to control the thinking and train of thought until the listener is attempting to live out the very actions that are being rapped about. The listener imitates the images they see. This enters into their heart and spirit and continues to germinate. A great proportion of you have acted out some of the violence that is contained in the lyrics of rap music. Many of the lyrics in rap music glorifies the life of being a "baller" and big shot caller, but many of you know that seldom do the masses make it to the big league. The songs tell you to go out and get it anyway you can, but they never tell the real story about being killed or locked up, if you're lucky. They rap about a life that they do not live. If you want to be successful in life, you have to get educated and work hard for what you want. Taking to the streets is only a temporary fix which can and oftentimes does come with a huge price tag and sacrifice.

Let's take a look at some lyrics in rap music today, particularly in gangster rap.

Gucci
Future
Nikki Minaj
The Game
Young Jeezy
Lil Wayne
NWA: Fu'** da Police

Questions:
What do you think about these lyrics?
What do these lyrics mean?
Do you think the professional rappers know what influence their lyrics and videos are having on you and other participants? In what way?
Do you think professional rappers are being used by the record labels? In what way?
How does it make you feel when the listener is being mentally and spiritually sedated by gangster rap music for the money they receive from the big companies and from the sale of CDs?
Who came out with the first rap song?
What do you think gangster rap music is?
Do you think that some of the lyrics in rap music contain a form of subliminal subjections?

Do you think rap music and its lyrics influence the mindsets of the participant we see and hear about today in gangs?

Do you think rap music is creating violent behaviors in some of the youth of today?

If yes, why do you think this has happened?

Do you think that certain of the rap videos are violent videos?

Do you hear violent messages in rap music?

If so, what effects do you think it has had on you and others?

Does rap music persuade a portion of young adults into destructive mindsets of violence?

Is rap music contributing to the young person's mind toward violence, being a rapper, or a star, and/or the illusion of being rich and a gangster?

Do you think some rap music lure young people into a hypnotic state of mind while on drugs and alcohol?

Directions:

Speaking on the topic of megahertz is at the discretion of the staff member. This section can be overlooked if staff members perceive their students are not ready. Participants can move on to answer the questions below.

Lesson:

Now we will take a quick look at what a megahertz is and how it plays a role in music. You will study more about a megahertz, what is 440 Hz, which has been changed from 332 Hz to 440 Hz, and why, which is now your international frequency. You can also conduct an internet search of other vibration frequencies of megahertz and what they are such as 396 Hz, 417 Hz, 528 Hz, 639 Hz, 852 Hz, and their vibration frequencies and the influences the sounds have on the minds and spirits of the people.

Questions:
What is a megahertz?
Why do you think 332 Hz was changed to 440 Hz?
Does all music have the same megahertz?
If no, why does the megahertz change?
Is there a universal megahertz frequency?
If there is a universal frequency, what is the megahertz?

Education and Transformation

The Creation of Copycats

Directions:

In this section, participants will examine the copycat pattern. They will explore life in its different realities and the copy-cat's reality. Participants will come to understand what people are controlled and manipulated by, both the positive and the negative.

They will look at parents, relationships with other family and friends, drug dealers, gang members, music, and self.

After examining the fundamentals above, participants should now have a better understanding as to what their foundation should be built upon. They can then begin their layout for their foundation.

Lesson:

The copycat pattern is a pattern that individuals use to copy the actions and opinions of others. It is this copycat pattern that we witness in everyday life. Everyone has experienced being a copycat and not all that we copy is negative. You have to choose what and who you will copycat. Will you copy the actions or lyrics of gangster rappers or will you copy the actions of one of your teachers or coaches or even some worthy person at your place of worship? You have to decide. No one will decide for you until you make the mistake of copying the wrong actions of the wrong people and then society along with the law will decide for you. The very fact that you are partaking in this program means that you have already experienced society and the justice system deciding for you.

When you copy the actions of others and you allow yourself to be controlled by others, you are considered to be a puppet. Puppets are controlled by strings. Sometimes you can't always see the strings which control your actions and many of you are not even aware that you are being controlled. You think that you are acting out of your own self-will when you actually are not.

Questions:
What is a copycat to you?

Do you think that you are a copycat? Why or why not?

Now let's look at life in some of its different realities and the copycat's reality.

Character and wisdom are sculpted over time. They come with loss, lessons, and triumphs. They come after doubts, second guesses, and exploring unknowns. If there were a definitive path to happiness and success, everyone would be on it. The seeds of your progress are planted in your past failures. Your best stories will come from overcoming your greatest struggles. Your praises will be birthed from your pains. So keep standing, keep learning, and keep living.

Reality is the state of things as they actually exist, rather than as they may appear or might be imagined.

Questions:

Where and how do you think your reality started?

What do you think your reality is now?

Realities:

Realities come in many sub-forms such as your senses or physical reality which we shall call your main or dominant reality. This is the reality that many of you operate out of on a daily basis. What you wear, how you look or present yourself, what you think and feel, and all of your physical being covers this main reality. Copying others presents itself in your lives in imitating the look of others such as rappers and other famous people. Who are you trying to look like other than yourself? Are your feelings your own or the feelings of others? The foundation of a positive reality comes when you commit yourself to living a positive and healthy existence. You must decide that you want to think, act, and interact with others in a healthy coexistence. It is totally okay to be who you are. You can make the necessary changes to become the successful person that you want to be.

There is also the reality of ideal relations. These are the connections that you form outside of yourself. What may be an ideal relation to you may not be a healthy relation for you. Some of your relations may be looked upon as a negative relation to others. More than likely, if a relation feels good to you, you will continue this relation rather it's a positive or negative relation. Many of you may put more feeling than necessary into different relations and this are not always a good situation for you. You have to ask yourself what having a relation with certain people will do for you and how they will enhance your life. You must know whether or not you are forming or have a genuine relation with the people you allow in your life. Not everyone you encounter is meant to be a part of your life.

Make a list of all the people whom you have a healthy and positive relation with.

Make a list of all the people whom you have an unhealthy and negative relation with.

<u>Healthy</u>   <u>Unhealthy</u>

Idols:

Idols are another reality for many of you. Choosing good idols is not always easy for you. Considering many of the pressures that you are facing today in your lives, you should always be very selective in who you choose to look up to and be a part of your existence.

Let's look at some of the negative idols in your lives.

Gang-bangers…Many of you have personal ties and relations with gang-bangers. Some of you even emulate some of the gang-banger's actions. You see gang-banging as being cool or you may even feel a certain personal connection of family with some of these bangers. Some of you may have family members and close friends who are bangers or you are a banger yourself. Being a gang-banger is a losing situation. No good will ever come out of being a gang-banger or being affiliated with gang-bangers. Bangers always end up dead or locked up. The choice is all yours on how you will groom yourself for success.

Gangster rap music and videos... Gangster rap music and videos are now shown on the Internet, cell phones, television, and other social media outlets. The music and the videos of rappers are very prevalent and accessible to young people today. Gangster rap and its violent music and videos can cause unconscious seductions which can be released onto the young adult mind as subliminal suggestions.

Many video games, rap music, music videos, movies, news, and pornography can work negatively on your subconscious. Considering some of your living conditions, unemployment, housing, welfare, and other stresses that have negatively impacted you, you need to be wise about what the messages are that you feed your brain. These stresses combined with constantly listening to gangster rap music and watching these videos are sometimes what influences you to become angry and violent.

When you listen to certain violent music, play with certain violent video games, and watch certain violent music videos, and other violent television shows, you begin to copy what you have fed into your mind. You begin to copy the negative actions and words of others.

You start to program yourself to become copycats. You become convinced in your own mind that the way you act and interact with others is reality. You must understand that this is not the reality of the world in which you live. You get out what you put in and if you feed your mind, soul, and spirit with violent and negative things, then that is what you will get back in return. You have the power within yourself to change what goes into your mind, spirit, and soul. You have the ability to change your life in to what you want it to be.

Violent video games... Violent video games have become the norm in most of your lives today. These violent video games are very dramatic and are being marketed to serve you in a way that will make you feel elated upon moving from level to level. The fact that you can interact with other gamers from all over the world adds a new flavor to the mix. Many of you have become the target of the video game companies that produce and sell these violent video games. It's all about the "Benjamin'" with these companies. They feed upon your desire for thrill. You have to decide what it will be about for you. You have to make good choices in what you choose to partake in.

Television... Television is one of the most dominant social media outlets in the world today. Imaging the world of sex, drugs, and violence, television will have you to believe it is okay to be involved in such
activities as these. Many of you have been programmed and don't realize how or why. The images from watching television develop in your subconscious mind leading you to be or do what is suggested from what you have watched. The negative information, which is fed to the public, is seldom confronted or opposed. This kind of information is psychologically harming American youth. You set the image for your own life. You must become the author of your success.

Athletes... Many of you look at certain athletes as role models. Some athletes have had trouble in their careers and have not been good role models for the youth of today. Some athletes even endorse products and services that are detrimental to harming many of you. With that being said, many of you still try and copy the actions and behaviors of your favorite athletes. Any negative behaviors that you copy of a famous or well-known athlete that influences you in a negative fashion, will only spell trouble for you. Groom yourself for success and turn all your negatives into positives.

Entertainers... Entertainers, especially gangster rappers, are a prevalent part of the your lifestyle. Young people try to imitate the lifestyle of their favorite entertainers. They copy their fashions, wanting to live the lifestyle that they believe the gangster rappers live. Social media outlets display entertainers to the world in the form of videos, television appearances, magazines, newspapers, the Internet (Facebook, Twitter, Instagram, Black Planet, Yahoo, Google, etc.). You have to understand that the copycat thinks that what they see on different media outlets glorifying entertainers is real. It is not real and it is a bad choice to make negative entertainers a part of your reality. You should never copy the actions of anyone who is negative. You must see life for what it is. You have the power to make your life a success.

Let's look at some of the positive idols in your lives.
Rap music and videos... There are positive rap music and videos available that carry with them a positive and uplifting message to young people. This music encompasses the same great beats found in gangster rap and will be a great fit for those who choose to feed their brain with a positive message. You will still enjoy the beats. You must remember that you are now a leader and you set the tone for your life. The tone you set can also be a positive influence on others' lives as well. You must make sure that the tone you set for your life is one of being true to who you groom yourself to be and staying on the road to success. You need always have structure in your life. Know what you want for your life and set your goals high.

Video games... There are many video games that offer up a wide variety of excitement that you can use for entertainment in your everyday life. Many of these video games aid you in building different skills during the interaction. They also contain positive material. Trying new video games such as foreign language, history, cooking, and the arts are just some of the many different varieties of games that will give you hours on end of fun. Discover what your entertainment needs are and why. Tailor your needs to fit you and showcase your leadership abilities.

Music and television... There are tons of different music and television programs that are available to you which will satisfy your tastes and give you something of positive value in your life.

Television offers many different genres of programming choices from science programs, cooking, history, wild life, government, aquatics, fashion, the arts, and much more. You can choose music that resonate a positive vibe for you. Choose to be unique and special to yourself and the world around you. Live your life to your full potential today.

Athletes... There are many profound athletes who have a positive self-image and live a good and healthy lifestyle that is not based upon illusions or copying others. There are numerous athletes who possess their own unique talent. They have discovered and developed their gifts. You, too, possess many unique talents. Sometimes you have to get up from under the surface to bring your special talents outward. You have a special gift in you that must be discovered. It is a gift that only you possess and is tailor made for you. Find the hidden gift in you.

Entertainers... You are all aware of the fact that there are many positive role models in the entertainment industry. Copying their lifestyle is not a good fit for you because you have to groom yourself for what works for you in the order of how you will accomplish your goals. You cannot dream someone else's dreams. Your roadmap for success will differ from everyone else's. You are a unique and special person who has to travel your own road to success. You will meet and form bonds with many different people along your journey to success. You should understand that some people are only supposed to be in your life for a season. You can overcome the challenges that you face today. You are a winner. Life will reward you when you begin living a healthy lifestyle.

Questions:
Who are your idols?
Are your idols a positive or negative influence in your life?
Who do you admire in your life? In your community? In the world?

Do you have any role models? Why or why not?

Friends and Associates: The Pros and the Cons

Here you should write out who your family, close friends, and associates are and examine the pros and cons of those relations. Don't worry about names. You can use numbers in place of names if you are not comfortable putting down a name. This exercise is about you. It is designed to give you a good look at the people who are a part of your immediate environment. You get to scrutinize what you put into and get out of having a relationship others. You can see the things that you would like changed in those relationships or even how you would like those relationships to move forward. Some of these relationships will be healthy and some will not. You have to choose which relationships will be good for you and which ones won't. It will be up to you. It's time for you to start to put major life changes into practice in your efforts to start to live a healthy lifestyle and begin being Groomed for Success!

Pros
Cons

What is your definition of a friend?
What is your definition of an associate?
Do you have a lot of friends and associates?
After writing out your pros and cons about your friends and associates, will there be any changes on your lists?

The Strings:

Control: 1. to exercise restraint or direction over; dominate; command
       2. to hold in check; curb: to control ones emotions.

Manipulate: 1. to manage or influence skillfully, especially in an unfair manner: to manipulate people's feelings.
2. to adapt or change to suit one's purpose or advantage.

The strings connected to the puppets/copycats, which oftentimes controls and manipulates your mental conditions, are seen through your physical actions. These strings are invisible to the physical eye but are directly related to and/or connected to your behaviors which orchestrate a large part of your life and the implementation of your daily activities.

You live in a society where different people control different areas of your life every day in society and so it is with all people living in society today. There is a major difference in the strings in your life that you have no control over and the strings in your life that you do have control over. Strings such as government, city, federal, state, and other laws of society are strings that you do not have any control over. How operations are conducted on your job and how operations are run in your religious institutions are other areas of your life that you more than likely wouldn't have control over. You do, however, have power over the very controls and manipulations that have been in placed in your life since your upbringing. You have the ability to change at this very moment and the decision is all yours. It is all about who you are copycatting in your life. If you are trying to copy the lifestyle of some of the negative people and things in society that we discussed earlier, then you are not exercising your ability to groom yourself for success.

Questions:
Who do you copycat?
What control and/or manipulates you?

Building Healthy Relations:

You need to take a long and thorough look at all of the information and topics in this program because it is specifically designed to change your life. You can and will have the life that you want and you will work toward that life one day at time, knocking down one goal at a time. It takes a whole lot of energy to copy another person or thing. Why waste such energy? You can use that energy to set your own roadmap to success into play. Begin to go after the things you want in life.

Each person who you encounter in your journey will be different and will leave different impressions on you. It doesn't matter what the profession or title held, you must tailor your family, friends, and immediate associates to fit your needs and wants. People will enter and exit your life like a revolving door and that's okay because, as we stated earlier, not everyone is in your life for all times. For the people who are a part of your life for long periods of time or indefinitely, you need to have healthy relations and communications with those individuals. Healthy relationships consist of love, trust, dependability, honesty, and respect, just to name a few. Give what you expect in return and even if you don't get back what you thought you should get back, give anyway.

Healthy relations with family and friends are what will be a vital part of your growth. If you don't have family and/or close friends, then you will create close friends and a surrogate family. These are the people who will love and care for you through the good and the bad, whom you will do the same for. You have to nurture the relationships that you want to have with others and it must be give and take. Try to gain relations with people who compliment you or that you compliment. Barriers are a good tool to use in forming and maintaining relations because it develops respect and understanding for all parties involved. Always set barriers in your relationships with others.

Questions:

How will you begin to begin to build your healthy relations with others?

What barriers and boundaries will you put in place?

The basic core practice in your Groomed for Success program is love and respect. You have to get up every day and make a conscious decision to treat people right, regardless.

No one can control you unless you give them control over your life. If you copy the negatives that you see every day in your life then you are basically giving over control of yourself to those controls, whatever they are. Many of you may feel like you were made to do certain things and certain things happen because you had no control, but when you look at your situations for what they really are, you had options that you chose not to exercise. Now you must exercise your options in making decisions for your life that work in your best interests toward you being "Groomed for Success".

The Plain Truth:

Being in a gang, affiliated with gangs, and exhibiting at risk behavior is a "no win" situation. It ends in death, jails, and institutions. Many of you are able to be tried as an adult and depending on the crime that you commit, you will be tried and sentenced as an adult and not as a teen. The criminal justice system is not playing around with young adult offenders in society today and each year more and more prisons and other institutions are being built to house you. You can change your life into whatever you want it to be or you can let others do it for you. The choice really is yours.

Directions:

Earlier in the lesson, participants wrote out pros and cons of the relationships they have. We will now look closer at some of those relationships with others. Here, participants will explain the type of relationship that they seek to have with the people whom they choose to have in your life. They will learn their actions with family will be different from their relations with friends and other professionals.

You will answer and examine six questions about each relationship. Remember, these are the people who will be in your life and you must be clear about the kind of relations that you want to move forward with.

In terms of the following, parents, siblings, aunts, uncles, cousins, close friends, associates, gang members, professional, religious, spiritual, the music, and self;

1. What type of relation do you want with this person?
2. What do you need out of this relation?
3. What you are willing to do to keep this relation?
4. Is it a healthy relation?
5. Is it a seasonal or indefinite relation?
6. Are there any barriers?

Building on a solid foundation. What is a solid foundation and how you can make that happen in your life?

A solid foundation consists of you surrounding yourself with people who love and respect you, and who you, in turn, love and respect. It also dictates you being able to go through your storms in life without giving up or giving in. In life you are going to have many trials and tribulations and ups and downs, but it is at these times that you must persevere. Part of your foundation will also include setting certain standards in your life, as well as, barriers for yourself and others. You must hold fast to the standards that you set for your life. Your decisions must always be for the truth and the good of your own personal success and others. You can only want success for yourself when you truly hope it for another. You must also utilize the resources that are available to you without shame or pride. Remain true to who you are and love and respect yourself and others. Always know that the key to your success is you.

You may want to start by building close relations with your immediate family and other loved ones. You will want to build your success on a solid network of people who have your best interest at heart, personal and professional. It is through your storms and trials and even good times that you must know you are not alone. Everyone needs an active and healthy support system because no one can make it on their own in this world. This is your time to build your support system.

You must next set standards and barriers for yourself and others whom you interact with. These barriers should include all family, friends, and professional relations. When making choices and decisions, you should always side with what the right thing to do is and do it. Practice honesty and truth at all times. Don't be swayed by others' ideas and struggles. Look at your own situations for what they are and be about your business of problem solving.

Always use the resources that you have and always be on the lookout for new and better resources. Always upgrade....never downgrade. You are the author of your success and your success looks like you want it to look.

Questions:

Write out the steps you will take to groom yourself for success and build your foundation upon.

What will you do?
Who will be a part of it?
Which resources will you utilize?

Education and Transformation

Gang Violence/At Risk Youth

Directions:

Participants will examine the effects of gang violence, gang affiliation, and at-risk behavior in depth.

Lesson:

There have been all kinds of movements in America for all kinds of rights, justices, and injustices and now there is a fight for the life of our youth. Our young people are committing crimes at an alarming rate. Countless of them are getting shot and killed, locked up for many years, and even being kept as sex slaves. A great proportion of the inner city youth who go out and commit crimes, join gangs, become affiliated with gangs, and exercise at-risk behavior usually have underlying issues which make them act and/or react to different situations.

You have to come to understand your history and address any issues in your past in order for you to be successful in your future. You have the freedom to choose the opportunities available to you to live within the laws of the land. Implementing the tools that you are learning from this program along with your own personal self-discovery, will enable you to map out a roadmap design entirely by you and for you. This roadmap is grooming you for success in life.

Gang Violence

The effects of gang violence are devastating to you and your community. Gang violence affects people everywhere. Both the victims and the perpetrators of gang violence lose, as well as their families, and all connected to them. A lot of you may know people who fell victim to gang violence, have perpetrated violence upon another, or even you, yourself, may fit into one or both of these categories. Violence of any kind is never an acceptable practice for anyone.

Gang violence is devastating for you because you can lose your life or go to jail and/or prison. You can also end up in a wheel chair for the rest of your life or worse. When you are in a gang or have close gang ties, family and friends are vulnerable to attacks from rival gang members. Retaliation is customary in the gang world. Your life is worth more than what any gang can ever offer you. You have to choose life because when you choose to be a part of a gang and have affiliations with bangers then you are choosing death. It does not matter how you go out, it is with certainty that if you do not give up the gang, stop banging, and get Groomed for Success, death and/or imprisonment awaits you.

Right here and now you are beginning a wonderful healthy life that will be filled with many different successes. You are making solid decisions about your life and the direction your life is going in. You must remember that in life you are always given choices and you are making good choices for your life.

Now you are growing up and growing out of some of your friendships and associations. It is not always easy to leave friends but you must remain the most important person to you. You are changing your issues into victories one issue at a time and as it was stated earlier, some of your past associates have ended their season in your life. You have to make room for the new. Everyone will not be happy about the changes that you are making in your life. Some will want to even challenge your new way but you must stay true to who you are grooming yourself to be. "To thine own self be true"! Knowing the causes and effects of being in gangs and or affiliated with gang members will keep you out of harm's way.

In bettering your lives you are making good and solid choices.

It is a fact that those who participate in the acts of gang violence will not last long in society. Mature young men and women handle their differences with dignity and respect, even in anger, always having love and respect for one another. You have to be aware of the war against other teens like you who are still out in your community and the city lost and feeling alone. You should never wish bad for your fellowman. You can only want success for yourself only if you desire it more for others. These young people, some you may know or see often, are still involved in gang violence. The same way that you have been offered a way out is the same way you should and could offer others around you a way out.

You have to know what is important to you in life. No one can decide what is important to and for you. No one can make you whole because you already are whole. You may feel broken and even fragile but you still are whole. In being a whole and beginning to make good choices and relations, you can no longer be afforded the excuse of others controlling your actions and behaviors. You are mapping out your POP (Plan of Production) now and you are gradually seeing the life that you want beginning to take form. You will have a complete road map in Phase 3.

No one can make you use drugs, join a gang, or go out and hurt or kill someone. No one can force you to make bad choices or make you exercise bad behaviors. You are given much of the same freedoms as others in society. You have choices as an individual and as a citizen of the United States. You also have the ability to choose positive or negative. Being involved with gang violence will never be a solution to any of your problems, ever!

Gang Affiliation

Many of you may think that it is okay to be affiliated or have ties to gang members. It is definitely not responsible nor is it wise to have affiliations with gang members. This exhibits a lack of poor judgment on your behalf. Lots of teens have been victims of violence leading up to death because of their affiliations with gang members. You may have friends and/or family who are in gangs or have strong gang ties. You will have to make some hard decisions about the people you have relations with who continue to participate in gang affiliation. The choices are all yours.

We realize that some of you may not be able to escape the affiliations of gang members in your immediate environment. Some of you have gang members in your families and family friends. Family functions make it hard not to be affiliated in some way in those types of situations. Remember, you can only set the boundaries that you can control. Know that exiting is always an option.

At-Risk Behaviors

Let us take a look at some of the different behaviors that young people participate in today. There are many different ways in which at-risk behavior is demonstrated by the youth. We will examine and discuss some of the main ones. Feel free to add others and we will discuss them also.

First, we will examine and discuss why sex is a major at-risk behavior for many of you. Being sexually active is considered to be okay by a lot of young people. Having sex at a young age creates a lot of different problems for the teen parents and other family members. It is usually the grandparents and other family who ends up raising and supporting the children of teenagers. Some of you already have kids who you are not able to provide for. These children are often the result of teenagers having unsafe sex.

Not practicing safe sex is like playing "Russian Roulette". You are taking a major risk with your life. You can contract many different sexually transmitted diseases (STDs) which can and/or cannot be cured.

STDs are illnesses that have a significant probability of transmission between humans by means of sexual behavior, including vaginal intercourse and oral sex.

Here are some of the common STDs that you contract from having unprotected sex: Chlamydia, Gonorrhea, Genital Herpes, HIV/AIDS, Human Papillomavirus, Syphilis, Bacterial Vaginosis, Trichomoniasis, and Viral Hepatitis. Some of these STD's are life-threatening because they are incurable.

When it comes to sex, you need to make decisions that will be healthy for the lifestyle that you are grooming yourself to live. Part of being a responsible young adult is making good choices for your life. You have to live with the choices you make. When you don't make good decisions and choices about sex, you will find yourself dealing with the consequences of your choices. When you allow yourself one moment of pleasure, that one moment can very well cost you for the rest of your life. Now you will have to start taking ownership for the decisions that you have made and will make in your future, whether good or bad.

It is wise to have set boundaries when it comes to sex. Having and sticking to the boundaries that you set affords you the opportunity to be in control of yourself. You don't have to participate because that is what it is cool or because others are doing it. You have to think smart about sex and your body just as you have to do in all areas of your life. It is okay to say "no" or to wait to have sexual relations. It is considered rather cool to be a virgin.

Drugs and alcohol is another growing epidemic with the young people today. Many of you have experimented with drugs and alcohol at some time in your lives. Drugs and alcohol does a lot of damage to your brain and physical body.

Marijuana is a very popular drug among young adults. Many of you smoke marijuana every day. There are many serious side effects that goes along with the use and abuse of marijuana. Of all the people who use marijuana, about one in eleven will become addicted. When a young person begins smoking marijuana in his or her teens, he or she has a one in six chance of becoming addicted.

The problems and effects related to you using marijuana are worsening mental and physical health, relationship problems, higher probability of dropping out of school or abandoning your goals, lower grades and reduced academic success, increased absences from school or work, and less career success compared to peers.

The short-term effects of using marijuana are sensory disorders, panic, anxiety, and poor coordination of movement, low reaction times, sleepy or depressed, and the risk of heart attacks.

The long-term effects of using marijuana are reduced resistance to common illnesses (colds, bronchitis, etc.), suppression of the immune system, growth disorder, increase of abnormally structures cells in the body, reduction of male sex hormones, rapid destruction of lung fibers and lesions, injuries to the brain could be permanent, reduced sexual capacity, study difficulties, reduced ability to retain information, apathy, drowsiness, and the lack of motivation, personality, mood changes and the inability to understand things clearly.

The withdrawal symptoms related to trying to stop using marijuana are irritability, insomnia, anxiety, nightmares, anger and fluctuating emotions, headaches, depression, loss of appetite, and craving to continuously use the drug.

Marijuana is not the only drug that many of you are experimenting with today. There is ecstasy, heroin, crack, cocaine, meth, oxycodone, hydrocodone, valium, Xanax, sleeping medication, and many other pills.

Alcohol is another major risk that teens are indulging in. Some of you may have already tasted your first alcoholic beverage and some of you still drink today. Alcohol really damages the body and can severely damage the brain. Let's look at what alcohol does to a young body such as is the case with many of you.

Alcohol affects every organ in the drinker's body and can damage a developing fetus. Intoxication can impair brain functions and motor skills, heavy use can increase risk of certain cancers, stroke, and liver disease. Alcohol abuse, which can lead to alcoholism, is a pattern of drinking that result in harm to one's health, interpersonal relationships, or ability to work.

You have to have boundaries for yourself when you encounter others who use drugs, alcohol, and/or participate in at-risk behavior. You need to keep yourself safe from these dangers at all times. You must give your mind the opportunity to develop as it should. This cannot happen when you are damaging your mind and body with drugs and alcohol. Drugs and alcohol do not fit into the life of a successful person.

Peer Pressure

Peer pressure and bullying are two issues that many of you may have experienced or might even be dealing with at this very moment. You need to be very clear about what peer pressure and bullying is. You need to be able to recognize peer pressure and bullying for what they are when presented to you and know how to handle yourself in the proper manner when dealing with one or both of these issues.

Peer pressure is influence that a peer group, observers or individuals exerts that encourages others to change their attitudes, values, or behaviors to conform the group norms.

Bullying is the use of force, threat, or coercion to abuse, intimidate, or aggressively impose domination over others. The behavior is often repeated and habitual.

Peer pressure occurs when your peers attempt to pressure you into doing or saying things that you feel uncomfortable with. Most of all teens experience peer pressure at one time or another in their lives. Peer pressure can come in many forms from different groups. Some of you have found yourself in jail, using drugs and alcohol, and in dangerous situations from choices you made because of being pressured into it by others. Many of these decisions were not decisions that you made on your own. Some of you are influenced by being cool or being daring. You want to fit in. Succumbing to the stresses of peer pressure is not in your best interest.

You need to learn how to handle peer pressure in the proper manner. The best way to respond to peer pressure is to politely and respectfully say, "No." It's okay not to fit in. It's okay to have your own style and way about yourself. If saying, "No" is not an option, then you need to have a plan B. You may want to consider speaking to an adult, counselor, or even the authorities. You must do whatever is necessary to keep yourself safe and on your road to success.

Bullying is an act of terror. There are many reasons why bullies do and act the way that they do and you need to learn how to deal with them. You must also try to understand why bullies use force and intimidation tactics. What this means is that bullies are very aggressive and demanding. Bullies are driven by violence. They are lacking something in their lives and they feed off of the negative popularity. You need to understand that negative popularity is not cool.

When you or any of your peers use force and intimidation on others, you are acting as a bully. You have no right to force anyone to do or say anything that they do not want to do. It is wrong to bully others for their belongings. Bullying is against the law.

Understanding the reasons why others bully people will help you to better understand how to deal with bullies. Some of the reasons why kids become bullies is because of low self-esteem, coveting, jealousy, envy, arrogance, self-centeredness, depression, and anger. There are many other reasons but these are just a few.

Questions:
List several reasons why you think people bully others.
Have you ever been bullied? Why?
Have you ever bullied others? Why?

Dealing with Bullies:

Knowing the correct methods to use in dealing with bullies is simple, stay away from them. No one can force you to do anything that you don't want to do. Tough guys and girls (bullies) don't last long. These people will always run into someone tougher than they are. If you befriend bullies, then those bullies will make decisions for you. You will sometimes have no choice but to do whatever they tell you to do. In grooming your life for success, you have no time for bullies and their negative energy. Bullies lives are controlled by how much power they can assert over others. You must never give your power over to anyone.

If you are not able to stop someone from bullying you then you must let an adult know immediately. Inform your school counselor, principal, and the authorities. You must be brave enough to take a stand against bullying. This should be included in your POP, (Plan of Production.) Bullying is wrong!

If you are the perpetrator of bullying then you need to stop immediately. You need to speak with a counselor right away. You need to discover the real reasons why you bully others. You need to change your actions. This should be included in your POP, (Plan of Production).

Resources:

Call (888) 248-0822
National Bullying Prevention Center
The End of Bullying Begins With You.
Pacer Center, Inc.
8161Normandale Blvd
Bloomington, MN 55437
Bullying and Cyberbullying
(800) 273-8255 Text ANSWER to 839863
24 hours a day, seven days a week
http://crisiscallcenter.org/crisisservices.html

Education and Transformation

Gangs Birthing Gangs

Directions:

The staff member will examine and discuss what a gang is, the orbiting cycle, attractions and objects of desires, the hazards of at-risk behaviors, and sexual relationships. They will also explore the theory of "Why gangs?". Program participants will take an in depth look at what gangs really are and how they came to exist. They will also have two mandatory readings relating to the subject matter and a mandatory reading selection entitled, "Dropouts".

After participants have read the two pamphlets, "20 Ex-Gangs and Gang Members Tell Their Stories and Give a Solution to Gang Violence" and "Gangs Before Thrasher", participants must answer the following questions and will need to explain all of their answers in detail.

Gang:

A gang is a group of recurrently associating individuals or close friends with identifiable leadership and internal organization, identifying with or claiming control over territory in a community, and engaging either individually or collectively in violent or other forms of illegal behavior. Some criminal gang members are "jumped in" or have to prove their loyalty by committing acts of such as theft or violence. Although gangs exist internationally, there is a greater level of study and knowledgeable information of gangs specifically in the United States. A gang member is called a gangster.

Gangs have been around for many centuries and still exist to this day. Currently, we have many different gangs in the United States. These gangs seek to control their immediate communities with acts of violence and illegal activities.

Many of these gangs such as the Aryan brotherhood, the Spanish cartels, the Asian mafia, the Black mafia, the Italian mafia, the Jewish mafia, motor cycle gangs, skinhead gangs, the Ku Klux Klan, and other gangs in America are very prevalent in society today. These gangs consist of all nationalities, races, and ethnic groups. These gangs are violent and have no respect for the safety of the people in their communities. They do not adhere to or obey any of the laws of the land. Their only interest is in furthering the cause of their gang. Oftentimes their cause is about controlling the streets, money, and drugs in their area.

The Orbiting Cycle:

What we will refer to as the orbiting cycle is the center of attraction and the objects of desire that lure you into joining gangs, being affiliated with gangs, and exercising at-risk behavior. It is the sphere of influence that a group or another person can have over you. These attractions and desires can be in the form of wanting to be a part of a family, peer pressure, identity, protection, fellowship, intimidation, attention, excitement of gang activity, financial benefits, family tradition, and a lack of realization of the hazards involved in being in a gang, affiliated with a gang, and exercising at-risk behaviors. Some of you were adopted and some of you may not have family. You think that joining a gang will give you what you lack from not having a family. You think that you will get what you desire from the gang. This is not the case. Joining a gang can never fill that void. You can create a healthy group of close friends and contacts who can act as family to you.

Questions:
What is the center of attraction(s) for you?
What are your objects of desire?
What do you think you will gain or lose by joining a gang?
How will you go about building a healthy network of close friends and family?

Peer Pressure

Peer pressure is something that many of you have experienced or witnessed firsthand. Living in your neighborhoods with the fear of not being connected to a gang can pressure you into joining a gang. Sometimes you may suffer dire consequences for not joining a gang. Many young people have lost their lives because they refuse to get with the "neighborhood program" by becoming a gang member. You all know how gang members think and feel about outsiders and others who are not a part of their clique. Many of these gang members know you and grew up with you but when it comes to pressuring you to be in their gang, it doesn't matter who you are, how long, or how well they know you, there is only one agenda that matters, that's you becoming a member of their set. It is never a wise decision to join a gang.

Questions:
Have you ever experienced peer pressure? In what way?
Have you ever witnessed peer pressure on others? In what way?
Have you or someone you know suffered any consequences for not joining a gang? What were the consequences? Explain.

Identity Crisis:

Many young people today suffer from an identity crisis. They are not sure who they are or what they want out of life. They are unsure of themselves and where they fit in their immediate communities and society. When you don't have your own identity, you tend to take on the identity and ideals of your family, friends, and associates. It is then very easy for you to be drawn in to becoming a gang member and displaying at-risk behaviors. You are now establishing your own identity.

Questions:
Do you think that you suffer from an identity crisis? Explain.
Do you know who you are? Explain.
Are you sure of yourself? Explain.
Do you know where you fit in your community and society? Where?
Have you ever taken on the ideals and beliefs of others? If so, who? Were these ideals and beliefs positive, negative, or both?

Joining Gangs for Protection:

Many young people who reside in low income disenfranchised communities feel that they have no protection or no one to look out for them in their neighborhoods. These feelings sometimes lead them to join gangs or keep close ties with gang members. They experience a feeling of safety with the gang behind them. You will come to understand that gang protection is not protection at all. It is something that you never need in your life at any time. You have the ability to protect and keep yourself safe from all hurt, harm, and danger at all times.

Questions:
Do you have someone to look out for you in your community?
Do these individuals have a positive or negative influence in your life?
If you were or are in a gang, what do you get from the gang?
What do you think about gang protection?
Is there a price that you have to pay to be protected by the gang?
How do you plan to keep yourself safe from all hurt, harm, and danger in the future?
What will you do to achieve this plan?

Fellowshipping

Fellowshipping for young people is about being a part of something larger than themselves. It is important that you always understand exactly what the group that you are a part of is all about.

Negative fellowshipping is never a good choice for you. You are now being groomed to fellowship with others in a positive and productive manner. You are in the process of building long lasting positive relationships.

Questions:
Which groups are you a part of or belong to?
What did you have to do to become a part of the groups that you belong to?
Do you understand what these groups are all about?
Of all the people that you fellowship (interact) with (including family), how do you view these interactions?
What needs to change about these interactions?
How will you select the people whom you interact with?
Which criteria will you use?

Intimidation

Intimidation is a tactic used by many gangs to exude fear and pressure upon you and others to get you to do what the gang wants you to do. It is also used to get you to participate in at-risk behaviors such as using drugs, alcohol, exercising daring and foolish behaviors, and having unprotected sex. You don't have to be intimidated by anyone any more.

Questions:
Have you ever been intimidated by another person? Why?
Have you ever intimidated others? Why? Explain.
Has intimidation led you to participate in at-risk behaviors? Explain.
Has intimidation ever caused you to use drugs and alcohol? Explain.
Do you understand what "subtle intimidation" is? Explain.
Have you ever been influenced by subtle intimidation? Explain.

Attention Starved:

Wanting to be the center of attention or not getting enough attention from family, friends, and other loved ones, puts many of you at a great risk for joining gangs and having the desire to "fit in". Many of you thrive off of attention and oftentimes it does not matter whether the attention is positive or negative. You may feel that you just need someone to pay attention to you. You act out because you think that no one cares. You need to always focus on and seek out positive attention and not the negative. There are people who genuinely love and care for you.

Questions:

Do you enjoy being the center of attention? Why?

Do you crave attention? Why?

What kinds of attention do you crave? Why?

Do you get attention from family, friends, and loved ones? How much? Is it enough?

Have you ever felt like you didn't fit in? Why?

What made you feel that way? Explain in detail.

Have you ever acted out just to get attention? Why? What did you gain?

Have you ever felt like no one loves or cares about you? Why?

Do you have people in your life who truly does love and care about you? Who are they? How do you know that these people love and care about you?

If you do not have people whom you feel loves and cares about you, how will you build your network of family and close friends? Who would these people be and what will they bring into your life?

Which criteria will you use to choose them? Explain.

Illusion or Reality:

Many of you love the excitement and illusion of participating in the negative activity and risky behaviors of being a "so called" thug, being in and affiliated with a gang, and exercising at-risk behaviors. On the contrary though, there are a lot of positive activities that you can participate in and learn from. These activities can also be enjoyable to you and your friends. Positive activities are very relaxing and motivating. You don't have to worry about negative feelings in a positive atmosphere because positive atmospheres position you in a right frame of mind. Changing your negative attitudes and behaviors into positive attitudes and behaviors is the main reason why you are being Groomed for Success. You always have a choice to exercise good morals and character and be positive. You are a winner.

Questions:
What is the thrill of the excitement for you?
What do you get out of that thrill?
Do you think that the negative activities and risky behaviors you have exercised in the past were more of an illusion that you were attempting to live out or was it all for excitement? Explain in detail.
What are some of the positive activities that you will participate in now?
How will you deal with friends and family who want you to go back to your old behaviors?
What plan will you put in place? Which barriers will you set?
How exactly will you change your negative attitudes and behaviors into positive attitudes and behaviors?

Financial Benefits:

There are financial benefits gained by being in a gang, having gang affiliations, and exercising at-risk behavior. You need to understand that these benefits are short lived. You have to sacrifice a part of yourself to attain these benefits and most times the sacrifice is not worth the benefit. Oftentimes many people suffer from your desire to gain financial benefits that you were not willing to work for. Hurting others for financial gain is never the answer. Working and earning an honest living for the necessities that you need and want in life is the proper way to go about fulfilling your every desire. Living as productive members of society is the way for you.

Questions:

What has been the financial benefits that you have gained from being in a gang, gang affiliated, and exercising at-risk behaviors?

What exactly have you given up for a few dollars, some name brand clothing, jewelry, or some other items that you desired?

Have you ever hurt or harmed another person while trying to gain any kind of financial benefit?

Have you ever been hurt or harmed while trying to gain any kind of financial benefit?

Family Traditions:

When we speak of family traditions we are speaking of the participant who have family members who are in gangs, have strong gang affiliations, and those members who display negative at-risk behaviors in the presence of the participant. These are individuals who you oftentimes must deal with and be around whether you want to or not. Many of these traditions and negative behaviors that your family members display have been placed upon you without consent. It is a way of life in some families. It is what your family does and it is what you have been taught to do. As you grow older, you may come to realize that the behaviors that you have been taught and those that you copy from family is wrong. It is most times difficult to break away from family who is negative. You have to learn to set boundaries for yourself when it comes to family and friends. You do not have to be like your family members or friends. You are defining who you are right now. You are one of a kind and you possess the strong and desire for success.

Questions:

Have you or anyone you know been initiated into a gang by their own family members? What was the outcome?

Do you have any family members who belong to a gang? How does that make you feel?

Do you have family members who exercise at-risk behavior in your presence and the presence of other young people? How does that make you feel?

What are your feelings about gang activity right now? Explain.

What are some of the traditions that you have been taught concerning the "streets" and "gangs"? By whom?

How do you feel about the negative behaviors you have been taught in the past?

How difficult would it be for you to sever ties with family that has a negative effect on you?

How would you accomplish that separation?

Who would you like to be like?

Who is your ideal person?

How do you see yourself now?

Realization of Hazards:

There is a lack of realization of the hazards of gang activity. It is comparable to quicksand. Some would say it's like sinking into a lifestyle and mentality of violence, destruction, and darkness. The most serious and main hazard from participating in gang activity is death. Jails and institutions are other hazards, along with teenage pregnancy. Becoming addicted to drugs and alcohol and other vises are some other serious hazards. These hazards are born out of your lack of realization and action when it comes down to you making serious life choices about being in, being affiliated with gangs, and exercising at-risk behavior.

Question:

What are the hazards of being in a gang, being affiliated with gang members, and displaying at-risk behavior for you?

There are so many different hazards that can come from you participating in at-risk behaviors. Drugs, alcohol, and sex are three of the main vises that go along with at-risk behaviors. Becoming addicted to drugs and alcohol can cause you and your loved ones a lifetime of pain and misery. Having sex at a young age and having unprotected sex is something that you should not be participating in. It's that simple to say, "No". You are worth waiting for. Even if you have already had sex or are currently having sex, you can still rearrange your sexual priorities and desires to fit into your healthy lifestyle. Although we strongly encourage you to refrain from all sexual activity at this time, if you feel that you cannot refrain from sexual intercourse, you need to set barriers and boundaries for your sex life.

Waiting until you are mature and responsible is your best bet. Your desire should always be to educate yourself, love yourself, remain positive, show kindness and respect, be accepting of who you are, and always be your brothers and sisters keeper.

Questions:

What are your at-risk behaviors?
What will you do to change them? Explain in detail.
How do you feel about sex? Explain in detail.
What are your thoughts about having sex at a young age?
What are your thoughts about having unprotected sex?
Can you remain abstinent for all at-risk behaviors? Explain.
How will you accomplish this?
Do you think that it is in your best interest to wait until you are mature and more responsible to have sexual relations? Why? Explain in detail.
What are your desires for your life?
Are you your brothers or sisters keeper?
What does that mean for you?

Education and Transformation

Why Gangs?

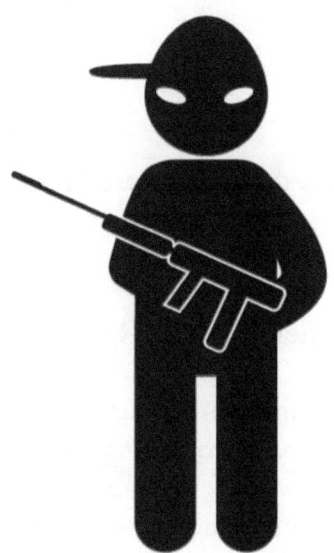

Introduction:

There are many different reasons why gangs exist. You will now take a look at why and how gangs came to be. The first gangs were started in New York in the 1800's. In the early days the word hang referred to a group of workmen and in the United Kingdom, the word is still often used in this sense, but it later underwent a pejoration. In current usage, it typically denotes a criminal organization or else a criminal affiliation.

Directions:

Participants will now read over and discuss the "Gangs Before Thrasher". Participants will then read over and discuss the "20 Gang Members and Ex-Gang Members" section of this book. To conclude this unit, participants will read over and discuss the "Dropouts" section.

After reading the first two sections, have participants answer the following questions. They will need to explain all of their answers in detail.

Questions:

What do you think the chances are of you falling into one of the 3 categories, being in a gang, being affiliated with a gang, and/or at-risk behavior?

Gangs Before Thrasher By Gang Research

"The word "gang" comes from "gonge" a term originally meaning a journey, but later referring to a gonge of sailors in the fifteenth century. Gangs of outlaws or wild young men came into common usage by Shakespeare's time. The Father of Gang Research, Frederic Thrasher, gave the word its industrial-era meaning in the 1920s and made gang into a term which meant "kids of the street" but US gangs had other predecessors than unsupervised street urchins.

There are four kinds of gangs which were predecessors of the street gangs of today. 1. Secret Societies; 2. Gangs of Outlaws in the Wild West; 3.Racist gangs like the Klu Klux Klan; and 4. Voting Gangs tied mainly to the Democratic Party in large cities.

1. SECRET SOCIETIES

Two Secret Societies are especially important for US gangs, as well as gangs around the world. Both the Chinese Triads and the Italian Mafia and Camorra have existed at least since the early 1800s.

Triads had their origin in anti-Manchu resistance in China, the term "triad" coming from the three dots which form part of the Chinese character for the Ming Emperor Hung Wu. Triads began as "Men of Hung." They were both part of the political resistance of the Han Chinese to the Manchu dynasty, as well as outlaws who "*Ta fu-chih p-'in*" (Hit the Rich and help the poor).

Triads spread all over the world and control much of the illegal and informal economy in overseas Chinese communities. Thrasher wrote about "tongs" in Chicago, defining *tong* as "protective society." The largest was the On Leong that also had chapters in New York and San Francisco

The Mafia also is made up of extended kinship groups. These groups originally maintained an ideal of manliness developed during the 1600's, when Sicily was ruled by Spain. The ideal called for refusal to cooperate with authorities and self-control in the face of hardships. In personal quarrels, a Mafioso took the law into his own hands and gained respect by using violence. Any offense might trigger a campaign of vengeance called a vendetta.

Mafiosi unofficially ruled part of western Sicily in the 1800's and early 1900's. Similar crime groups, such as the Camorra in Naples and the Onorata Societa (Honored Society) in Calabria, developed in other parts of Italy. The Black Hand was a secret society which practiced extortion on Italian immigrants.

The Black Hand were responsible for large numbers of murders in Chicago in the early 1900s: 10 in 1910; 40 in 1911; 33 in 1912; 31 in 1913; and 42 n 1914. The Mafia never really developed in Chicago, as it did in New York or Boston. By the mid-twenties, Capone had turned Torrio's vice operations into what is known today as the "Outfit."

2. OUTLAWS IN THE WILD WEST

As the cities were growing in the 19th century, the wild west spawned a male culture of violence. This male culture included the gold rush of 1848 where 90,000 men poured into California with a ratio of twenty men to every one woman. Rates of violence were astronomical, and an outlaw culture soon formed alongside the rough male culture of the gold fields.

The James Gang and many others have been the prototypical "gang" for America, up until the Capone years. Hollywood has had made a deep impression on Americans. The tough guy, cowboy culture of "shoot first and ask questions later" has been drilled into the American psyche.

The outlaw has a long history in other cultures as well. Gangs of "highwaymen" are written about in Ireland and elsewhere. Often people were seen as being forced to become bandits by "bad guys,", especially foreign oppressor. "Social bandits" like Robin Hood or Zorro were part of national resistance.

3. THE KLU KLUX KLAN AND RACIST GANGS

Many gangs of armed young men were racially motivated. Racial tensions in cities, like New York, were constant, and racist conflict was almost everywhere more violent and vehement than nativism. During the civil war, "draft riots" in NYC were thinly disguised anti-black Irish gang violence and about a thousand people were killed or injured and over a million dollars damages.

While competition for jobs was a source of hostility between many ethnic groups, no other group was so brutalized and dehumanized as Black people. Gangs of young men who fought each other over turf and honor, turned vicious and murderous when fighting Blacks. The "draft riots" were little more than a program.

After the civil war, the Ku Klux Klan arose as a "secret society " of men, and in the beginning not poor men, but former Confederate officers. The KKK institutionalized in the south as an extension of the power of the planters, part of the overthrow of reconstruction. The KKK was the violence of armed young men enforcing segregation and a racial order of domination in the south.

Racism was not the property of just the South. The final predecessor of gangs was what Eric Monkkonen calls "voting gangs" in New York City and the east. This was an Irish invention, using the pub culture of males to help the Irish become politically dominant. Gangs of roughs were encouraged, organized, paid by politicians to "help" in elections. Opponents were beaten up, voters intimidated, and voting booths destroyed and votes stolen.

It was these mainly Irish "gangs" which were the core of the draft riots of 1863. Chicago's Democratic Party formed "Social Athletic Clubs" modeled after New York's Tammany Hall thugs.

The famous clubhouse of the Ragin's Colts

In Chicago, the Democratic Party, already dominated by the Irish, borrowed the New York "Voting Gangs" custom and took them to new heights, or lows. "Social Athletic Clubs" were groups of young men, oftener of organized in sports and sometimes had clubhouses. Politicians used the SACs as they had in New York, to make sure the favored candidate won. In doing so, they built clubhouses for their favorites, and sometimes named the gangs after themselves such as the Ragen's Colts at right.

1919 was an ominous year. In cities around the US, returning soldiers used their weapons to put the blacks who had been recruited to the factories in the north as the war ended immigration, in their place and took their jobs back. Blacks, many of whom had seen social equality in France and had also kept their weapons, responded to violence by violence.

Major riots rocked East St. Louis and Chicago as Irish and other white ethnic gangs spear-headed the murderous assaults in both cities. Black gangs formed defensively and actively defended the Black Belt.

4. CONCLUSION: A TYPOLOGY

To summarize, before Thrasher, there were four types of predecessors to his gangs. 1. Secret Societies, like the Mafia, Camorra, and Triads; 2. Gangs of the Wild West and the tradition of highwaymen; 3. Racist gangs, like the KKK, which persisted from the end of the civil war to today; and 4. Voting gangs began in NYC and taken to violent heights in Chicago.

From this discussion, we can conclude that gangs then and now roughly fall out into four categories. 1. There are gangs of oppressed groups, which form because of lack of opportunity, and often take it by outlaw means (original Mafia; western outlaws); 2. There are gangs which are used by dominant or rising groups to enforce their power by violence or terror (KKK), voting gangs; some (Triad and Mafias); 3. There were gangs which lasted only a short time, usually until the leader is killed or grows up (James Gang; most social athletic clubs and urban gangs) and 4. Those gangs which persist for decades, and sometime longer (Triads, Mafioso) (Chicago's), (SACs), (the KKK). These gangs are said to have institutionalized, or taken permanent form.

20 Ex-Gang Members and Gang Members Express Their Feelings on Gang Violence and its Solutions

#1-"Hi, I'm Shawn, A.K.A little Swan. The only love I had during that time was the love for my dogs in our crew nothing else mattered, nothing else was important. The street life was the only way we knew and there was no other way. As I became conscious of myself, I became vulnerable to my feelings, to love, kindness, and to responsibility. These feelings I thought I could never have and I never wanted to have them.

What I learned from my experiences is how caught up I was in the illusion of gang banging. If someone could explain to me why at that time I depended on violence and believing in my crew, one would have the solution to the making of gang violence."

Question:

What do you think little Swan was going through? Was it the lack of love, poor parenting, peer pressure, or being in a neighborhood where gang violence was very prevalent and having to choose a side because where he lived?

#2-Micaiah A.K.A Oozy, "I started in my crew at the age of ten years old. I was initiated and brought into a hard core life. My crew was a lot of homeboys that accepted me and my crew was the most important thing to me in my life at that time. My dad was in the penitentiary doing nineteen years. I hadn't seen him in six years. My mother had to do what she had to do. I had two sisters and I admit my mother had it hard but one thing I didn't like is that she started smoking crack. I guess the pressure got to her too, taking care of three kids without a man.

Sometimes we see her out on the streets while my dogs (crew) and I were kicking it and standing around drinking beer. We would see her sometimes looking for crack. I would be so embarrassed. At times my dogs would tease me and say, "Say man, are you going to buy your mama a $10 sack from me! Yu know I got it!" I would get so mad at them and just walk away. I would not let anyone deal to my mom because I had crack too in my pockets and too ashamed to deal her crack. I wanted to hide my face because no one of my crew's mom was out on the streets looking for crack.

My solution to gang violence is this, we need jobs to make money to pay bills. Give us the chance to change and we will."

Question:

How would you feel seeing your mother or father out in the streets looking for drugs?

#3-"My name is Jonathan A.K.A J Boy. I started with my crew when I was eleven years old. I was told in my neighborhood I had to join the crew or stay off the streets because if they saw me they would hurt me or kill me. I found the love I was missing from my gang or family was the love that I was missing from home. My mother was never home. I started living with my two homey's (friends) from my crew by the time I was thirteen years old.

I thought they were all I needed. At the age of fourteen years old, I would be facing a murder because of my ignorance. When I was arrested, I realize the ramifications of my actions but when you are out there in the streets with the boys you do not care. You have no feelings for others only the crew. It feels like your sleep walking in a dream, listening to your music, smoking, and drinking but I woke up in jail.

To say I wished I could have made better choices or if I could turn back the hands of time, I would do it all different. What made me want to be in a gang in the first place was it the threats on my life? Now I'm doing life for murder. I'll never get out of jail. If I would have known now what I knew back then, I would have told you the solution to gang violence is understanding and the willingness to help the youth let go of their pains, trials, and tribulations in life. I would have been walking with an independent attitude in my community and a welcoming spirit of giving and not taking. The solution to gang violence is this, we must enlighten the youth about the dangers of the streets and gang violence. Man, this is a trip. I don't want to do life in here. I'm sorry."

Questions:

In certain neighborhoods in the bigger cities and in the ghettos of America you have to join gangs or the gang members will hurt or kill you. What do you believe?

If you believe this, this means some of the young people have no choice but to choose life or death at that time by joining these gangs. What do you think you would have done?

Now J-Boy is in jail for life, but at least he is alive or is he?

What do you think about J-Boy?

#4-"Trayvon that's me, but my street name is Hennessey. I was like one of the hit-men, you know that guy that take care of business when business need to be taken care of. They sent me when they wanted a job done right. Once I left, there was no compromising. There is a code of ethics and there is an honor that we keep toward one another and when the job is done we bring back proof.

I needed to know what was wrong with me. Why I enjoyed hurting people so much and why I was addicted to murder. I found the answer and I stopped. I had to move out of town from the place I grew up. I did not want that life anymore. I felt like the devil. I was so broken and so sorry for hurting those brothers and their families. Now I'm with the Lord in church. I ask for forgiveness every day for my past actions. Eight people are dead because of me.

The solution to gang violence is something that I never thought of. That's a good question but my solution would be going to the root of the problem. What is the root? Is it within itself? What kind of energy is behind gang violence? Gang violence is a negative energy and these young people have a lot of energy that need to be directed and housed in a positive direction. The real question is, when and where did it all start? Who created this foolishness? Who brought it to the streets to the youth today? Who cause this to happen? There is a solution. It starts with all of us. We must continue to keep the young people off the streets fighting each other and we must love each other and not hurt one another. Hurt and embarrassment has been a way of life that has been handed down to youth within ghettos and neighborhoods from generation to generation. The jails are filled with youth. The young people must change and be educated about the streets and gang violence. These young men and women need jobs. The youth are the solution and the future of America."

Questions:

What about the people he hurt?
What's wrong with this story?
What do you think?

#5-"Never mind my real name, I'm little Joe. I'm in my hood for life. My boys and I will never part. We will never separate from each other. We know our life is short that's why we live the way we do, as if there is no tomorrow, just today and today is our future. We have lost thirteen of our boys in two months. Seven were killed and six are doing life in jail. We take care of our boys in jail and we depend on each other. Our boy's girls (girlfriends) who they left behind in the streets after their death and jail sentences, most of the girls come to the crew for help and get with one of us. We take them in and give them to one of the boys who don't have a girlfriend.

You asked me what I think the solution to gang violence is. We do not want to stop banging. You would have to take all of us off the streets to stop us and you will not do that because we sell your drugs. We are you. We are what you made,. Stop us and then you stop yourselves from getting money. I buy from my leader who buys from some people in plain clothing. They supply him crack to sell for them. They are the solution but they do not admit this."

Questions:

We know there are bad people, but what do you think is the most important influence on the young person entering into gangs?

What do you think about Little Joe?

How would you feel about leaving loved ones behind?

#6- "I'm A.K.A Spanish Boy. I handle all the drugs. I'm responsible for that count and we have a program, how much drugs we give to each individual corner. We have three on a corner. Each one gets an ounce of crack a week. They bring $700.00 back and the other money they keep. Sometimes we help those in our crew to get some wheels (cars) or an apartment but that depends on how long they've been with the crew. We take care of each other. I have been in my crew for twelve years before I got tired of the problems. I've been shot two times, once in the back and once in the chest. I'm still here to tell my story.

I think the solution to gang violence is going to the real source. Where are all the drugs and guns coming from? We do not bring these drugs in to the hood in America. This problem starts with people who are involved, who are allowing others to bring drugs in. Do they want to keep people on drugs and flood the communities with drugs? We must stop them. To solve the problem of gang violence, we must stop the heavy hitters; the drug pushers.

Questions:

Who do you think are involved in supplying the drugs in our neighborhoods?

How can we do our part in keeping guns out of our communities?

#7- "I Am Diallo, A.K.A Little Lo. We got it going on and I run my set. I'm serving a life sentence for murder so I was given the role of the boss in the crew. I'm the one they knew should have got it anyway, (next in line for death). There were two attempts to kill me that failed. The jealousy and enviousness of some of the ones in our own crew was out there but we took care of the problems. They can't roll on me anymore, (try to kill me). It's about twenty-five of us tight and organized in our business. We are re-crewing every day, selling weed, heroin, and pills, you name it we got it and we do it! My solution to gang violence is this, give us what is coming to us, the things we need to get over. We need money to live. We need jobs just as others need work then we would not need to be on the streets."

Questions:

Will jobs help these young people off the streets? Some of them are very poor with no education at all, what kind of work could they do?

How would you deal with having to serve a life sentence?

#8-"I'm Leroy they call me Light. Our crew is different from many other crews. We are the neighborhood crew. We are all from the same hood. Nobody can come in or get out once they come in the hood. We are in for life, do or die. This is what you get being in the hood and coming in to the crew.

We are all doing good. Got our own places (apartments) and cars. We are one. We are about surviving. There are no jobs for us. Gang violence will always exist for the next twenty to thirty years or maybe longer because of the money and power that comes with it and we would rather die than to give this up! I am one of those people who would rather die. We are living in luxury and in class. You have to kill me to take what I have hustled for and my crew, that's the solution we are. We make the world go around."

Questions:

Do you think gang violence will always exist?

These young people have known each other all their lives but they shoot at one another and kill each other just because one group may live three to four blocks from one another and have a different crew. What do you think about Leroy?

#9- Alter' Ray A.K.A T- Bone, "I was fourteen years old when I came in the hood crew. I had to kill for my initiation. They showed me who, where, and how. Sometimes people owed the crew and they got tired of waiting for their money or sometimes they would just pick a person. (It was) unfortunate for that person but I didn't want to kill them but they may have killed me for being a punk or not knowing if I would snitch on them. So you were in or out. There is no middle; no straddling the fence.

We all have something on each other, a secret, some hidden murders, rapes, robbery, parole violations, probations violations, you name it. And we got it in the crew. The only solution to gang violence is this, doing what they should have done a long time ago, just stop it. They know how."

Questions:

How many innocent people have died from gang initiation?

How many unsolved murders do you think gang violence are involved in?

#10- Isaiah A.K.A Ice, "They call me Ice because I'm so cold hearted even to my family. The only ones that care for me is my crew. That's it and that's all. I wouldn't have it any other way. I'm not in school. I dropped out in the 8th grade when I was thirteen years old. I'm seventeen years old now. Selling drugs is the only way to make it in the hood, even though the sales of crack have slowed down.

People are getting clean in programs and in churches, talking about their higher power, having positive energy, gangs, and their violent activity. This is what their program and the churches teach them so money has slowed down a lot. We are the solution. If there was more control of administrative efforts to help the poor with jobs, violence would slow down in the streets and would be a little safer but it seems as if no one helps. We can't stop hustling and we have to survive like everyone else.

We don't need no books or anyone to tell us how to stop gang violence. We need more jobs for ourselves. If we can't find jobs, what do you expect us to do? We will keep hustling because we have to live just like everyone else have to live, eat, and sleep."

Questions:
What do you think Isaiah should do?
Do you think you have the choice to get a job or sell drugs?

#11- Hi I'm Sly, A.K.A Glock. That's all I carry. You have to know your friend, (weapon). You see, I know what a Glock can do and this is all I carry. I used to be where I want to be at a time in my life where I loved my crew. We did everything together, even murders but that's the past. I have turned over a new leaf in my life. I fell in love got married, have three kids, a good job, and a beautiful family. I have been on my own from the age of sixteen years old. If I can get out of my hood gang, anybody can. You just got to want it enough.

So you want to know the solution to the violence out in the hoods? These gangs are very serious about what they are doing and how they have to survive. They need money to live and some of them have families just like working people have families and gang members have dreams just as other people do.

My solution is this. They all need jobs and you can't put that many people in one place with no jobs and expect everything to be alright! They got to get out of their conditions. There are no jobs. It's like it has its own pull on you. You get stuck in the hoods and can't get out. Millions of them are in the hoods and can't get out. If they remove the problem, you can solve the problem of gang violence"

Question:

So Glock feels any one can get out of the gangs if they really want to, do you believe this?

#12- Daniel A.K.A, Scar Face, "When I was thirteen years old at school, I had a fight with two gang members and two of them after school jumped me. They called me, Pretty Boy, because I'm mixed (black and white race). They hated me, now they call me Scar Face. I was cut deep on my right cheek. Every time I look in the mirror, I see that day at school and it was all over nothing but jealousy and a girl. At that time, I wasn't in a gang even though I was leaning toward the gang that I'm in now. I got both of them. They won't be cutting anyone else.

The solution to gang violence is taking people like them out of the schools and off the streets. Maybe I was wrong for what I done to them. I just wanted revenge. I was not a bad person then but every time I looked in the mirror every day, that scar is what made me the person I am today. I'm twenty-three years old and I'm still in the gang, there is no way out. I just don't know. There is nowhere else to go but in my hood with my crew. The solution is this, stop the flow of drugs in the hood.

Questions:

Scar Face has a scar to remind him for the rest of his life of the two who jumped him after school. What do you think Scar Face should have done?

If he had told one of the facilitators at school or told the police, he would have been considered a snitch. What would you have done?

#13- "Hey, I'm Tommy, A.K.A Tray-D, It all started when I was about eleven years old. One day I was walking to school and two dudes approached me and asked me to run a package to somebody in the hood after school. Everybody knows each other in my hood and my mother and father was not together (divorced). My mother continuously hustled the streets and she was never home so she didn't know when I came home from school and I didn't think she cared. I told them, "Yeah I'll do it", especially when they told me I got paid $45 for a run every day. Three years later, I came all the way in the crew and took our oath; the initiation.

To be honest with you, I do not want to know the solution to gang violence. I'm just getting started but if they try to stop us, we would just hide; go underground. So you see, if we don't want a solution to gang violence there wouldn't be anyone to find for a solution. Well you might catch a few crews, those who retreat back to the streets to get their money, but we would just take it to a total different level where it can't be seen. The real solution to gang violence is stopping the drugs. They are killing over money and power to survive out on the streets because it's very hard in the ghettos. It's tuff out here just to survive."

Question:

How hard do you think it is to make it in the ghettos living around hundreds of people trying to hustle and work to survive to stay alive because the rate of unemployment is so high?

#14- "My name is Tray 'Shawn, A.K.A Hood Rat. I think the solution to gang violence is simple. Gang violence has been around for thousands of years. Groups of people who don't agree with systems and rebel against them, they blame the government or that system they disagree with because of their ruler ship, religions, and/or policies, or the lack of them. If we asked ourselves what they did to resolve the problems in the past, we can use the same methods or manipulations which gave them success in the past for a solution to gang violence today."

Questions:

Can the same methods and strategies be used to solve these problems of gang violence today?

How can we work together with the government to help end gang violence?

#15- "My name is Omar A.K.A "Chain". I was eleven and half years old when I saw my first murder. I was coming home from school. Sometimes it's dangerous walking through the parks. There is a lot of shooting that goes on there. It was three of us together that day. As we were walking in about the middle of the park, we heard loud talking. It sounded like they were getting ready to fight. As we looked over into the crown, a dude (guy) pulled out a gun and shot another dude (guy) three times in the chest.

We didn't understand what the confusion was about but the results sure wasn't good. Man, that was a trip to see somebody get blow away like that but it happens every day where we live in the hood. I wish there was a solution to gang violence. I wish somebody could do something about it. I was only in the gang for three years and had to get out of town. I owed a couple of my buddies (crew members) in the gang. I didn't have the money to pay them for the drugs they gave me to sell nor did they believe my story.

I was robbed for the drugs and the money. They thought I was lying to them and not wanting pay what I owed. I knew they would kill me and I did not want to die! The only way I see a solution to gang violence is to take everything off the streets, all the drugs that are being sold to the crack addicts, heroin addicts, and pill addicts off the streets and get them all help. Anyone caught selling drugs would do life in prison and anyone caught using drugs would also do a large sentence in jail which will help them to dry out and clean up while in jail. That's my solution."

Questions:
   Does 'Chain' have a good solution to gang violence?
   Will something like this work?
   Will there be enough room in the corrections facilities to hold the law breakers?

#16-Melvin A.K.A Storm, "My solution to gang violence will take time but it can work. Anyone associated with gang violence, gang affiliation, or has a record indicating gang involvement should have some type of sensor or chip in their body or on them telling their whereabouts and activities. With this device, monitors can hear the activities and plans; something which can't be taken off regardless how hard that individual tries.

Not only can you hear and see those individuals but this device can disable a person by pushing a button and give such a shock to where that person would not want to feel that shock again. Something strong enough if necessary to knock them unconscious and go arrest them right where they lay for planning criminal activities.

The person or gang member with this device cannot hurt anyone if they tried. A device which can monitor and hear the activities of individuals before they commit crimes, this is needed. This proactive device will give law enforcers a lot of straightening up from gang activities. I believe gang violence would decrease 80%.

Questions:
   Is a device like this ethical to put on felons and or gang members?
   Will something like this resolve gang violence?

#17- Timothy A.K.A Pit Bull, "I know the solution. If they legalize drugs, the gangs would not have a street corner to fight over. Within thirty days, violence would slow down a lot. Who are your drug lords? Who is in control of the drugs that come in America? We know who does this? It's their secret world that's doing all that we see and they allow this to happen.

We are dealing with greedy individuals. They should care more for human life not just material gain, power, and their riches. If you can arrest some of these people in these groups, you will have the solution to gang violence."

Questions:

Who do you think is participating or involved in drug trafficking in America?

What would do if you were faced with preventing drug trafficking?

#18- Kenny A.K.A Slice, "Every day we live the same activities over and over again. It's like a cycle you can't get out of. I've been doing the same stuff for fifteen years, selling drugs, robbing people, and in and out of jails. Now I'm a felon and it's on my record. It's hard. No one want to hire me so I do what I got to do to survive.

The only solution to gang violence is this, get to the ones with the big drug connections that own boats and air planes who put the drugs in the hoods. They need to stop! If you dig deep into the drug problems you will find men with their hands in the cookie jar with all the cookie crumbs on their hands."

Questions:

What do you think about Kenny's solution to help end our growing drug problem?

Most ghettos are not comprised of boats, airplanes, or factors to make such a magnitude of drugs being brought into our neighborhoods, how do we stop this?

#19- Cecil A.K.A, Assault, "When I started getting money on my block in my hood, I had to show the other gang rivals I was not playing about my money and I was not going anywhere because it's hard out there. It's rough in the hood. I had to do things I didn't want to do. I had no choice and today nothing has changed. Now I'm homeless. I'm broke, disgusted, and can't be trusted. My life is messed up! We live the way we live and keep things to ourselves because our business is just like the professional businessman and women of this world. Attorneys usually hang with attorneys, judges hang with judges, Congressmen go out with each other, so it's birds of feather flock together and so do we.

The solution to gang violence is this, go to the source, the ones who are the big drug dealers and suppliers. They need to be stopped and we all know who they are. So don't tell me that we have a problem with gang violence. We have a problem with millionaires and billionaires. They are dangerous and they're not going to give up those billions of dollars they make a year in drugs. They are the problem and they are the solution."

Questions:
Who are the drug suppliers?
Do you feel social or financial status plays a role in who you are around?

#20- "I'm Richard A.K.A Money. I been in my gang now seven years. The money has slowed down greatly. We had to find other ways to keep our money coming in so we started burglarizing people's homes, people that got money, jewelry, computers, and electrical equipment,. Anything that we see that may be worth taking.

You asked me about the solution to gang violence and what do I think about gang violence. Being a gang member for seven years, I know that sometimes we have to retaliate on other gang rivals. I know that sometime innocent people get hurt and yes, it is our fault for some of the street violence which goes on in our communities and neighborhoods but that's life as I know it.

You have to understand. If I had a job, if people would hire me and other like me, we would not be in a gang. I would be working like I was told to do by my parents. When I was younger, I had a robbery and it's on my record. I was eighteen years old I'm twenty-five years old now. I want to work. I'm so tired of being out in the streets watching people die and watching my friends die but they give us no choice but to survive out here in the ghettos.

The solution to gang violence is this. If they will put more money into the ghettos and make more jobs available, a lot of this violence and joining gangs would stop. We need help just like everyone else. We need money in the hood to survive."

Questions:

Do you think the American government knows how to stop gang violence?

If so, how do you think the government's approach will satisfy the needs of the American people in this violent condition we face today?

Do you believe what these respondents are saying about their experiences in life?

Are they a true reflection of how our young people think and act today?

Are you willing to be part of the solution to ending gang violence?

Why do young people join these gangs or choose to have at-risk behaviors'?

Why do you think that the youth today, knowing the danger of the streets, go out into the streets and participate in activities that will cause them to go to jail and receive lengthy prison sentences and oftentimes, death?

What do you think is behind the violent mind-set of the young person today?

What do you think happens to gang members?

What is the definition of the word "gang"?

What is the model of gangs?

Where did gangs start from?

How long have gangs been around?

Do you believe this negative mindset of the youth today has been handed down from the generations?

Do you think that the mindset of the young people today has been passed down from family or is it the result of environmental conditions?

Do you think poor living conditions are the cause of some gang violence?

Why do you think gang members don't have affection for one another or other people in society?

Do you think that young people are sometimes forced into gangs in order to survive? Why?

Dropouts

Youth from the ages of twelve through nineteen years of age have a high dropout rate. You cannot be in school full-time and progressing when you are involved in gang activity full-time. You will have to choose one or the other. It is being wise and preparing for your future when you choose to stay in school and get educated.

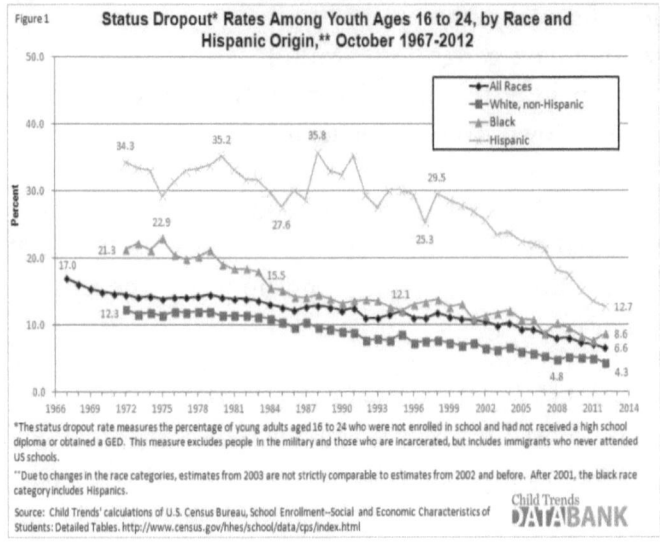

Questions:

Why do gang members drop out of school?

Have you ever dropped out of school or thought about dropping out of school? Why?

Have you ever been suspended or expelled from school? If yes why?

What do you think is the cause of you joining these gangs or participating in at-risk behaviors?

Young people must remain mindful, respectful, and focused at all times. Always be aware and observant of your surroundings.

Education and Transformation

Solution to Gang Violence

Directions:

Participants will now discover a solution to gang violence, gang affiliations, and at-risk behaviors. They will write out a solution to their own at-risk behaviors in detail. They will also write out an outline of the challenges they will face in keeping them from being in a gang, being affiliated with a gang, and participating in at-risk behaviors. Participants will start entering information from their notebook, mandated readings, and workbook into their Plan of Production (POP). 75% of the POP should be completed at this stage in the program. Participants will also begin to map out their Roadmap to Success (RTS).

The Solution Starts With You:

What do you think you can do to stop gang violence? You and your peers are a vital part of the solution to gang violence, gang affiliation, and at-risk behaviors. From your own life's experiences, you are able to develop, implement, and use the resources available to you to come up with your own solution to gang violence, gang affiliation, and at-risk behaviors.

Looking over your earlier writings, your self-discoveries, and the tools that you have been given from Phase 1, and where you are at now in Phase 2, you should have the necessary insights to come up with a solution to gang violence and at-risk behaviors. Knowing what happened to you and what brought you to the point in your life to be an at-risk youth, not only aids you in dealing with your own issues, but it will also help you to be a benefit to other at-risk youth.

It is important for you to stay out of harm's way. That means that you will stay away from gangs, gang affiliations, and at-risk behaviors. Each time you enter into the company of individual gang members, your life is in jeopardy. Gang violence is wrong, at-risk behaviors are wrong, and affiliating with gangs is just as dangerous as being in a gang.

You must see yourself as an important person in society with special talents in which Groomed for Success has assisted you in discovering. You can't become your brother's and your sister's keeper if you are in a gang and are continuing to practice at-risk behaviors. You are now embracing who you are and developing the gifts that you possess. You are one of a kind and you have something unique and special to offer society and the community that you live in.

Being Groomed for Success is a choice that you have to make for yourself. No one can make the decision to change your life for the better but you. No one can make you do right the right things in life. No one can make you use drugs, join a gang, go out and pull a trigger and hurt or kill someone, or exercise any other negative behavior. These are your own choices as an individual and it is at this very moment that you must decide that you want the best that life has to offer you and be willing to do whatever is necessary to be successful in life. Acting out of love, self-respect, peace, integrity, good character, and good decision making is what will free you from your past and give you a bright and healthy future. The choice is all yours.

Assignment:

Your writings for each subject matter should be at least two pages in length and detailed.
Write out your solutions to gang violence.
Write out your solutions to gang affiliation.
Write out your solutions to at-risk behaviors

Meeting Your Challenges:

You must meet the challenges of everyday life head on. Some of these challenges will not be easy for you to meet head on. You must discover a way to meet them regardless to whether you are still in a gang, still gang affiliated, or still displaying at-risk behaviors. Some of your greatest challenges will be clearing negative people out of your life and this may include close friends and family. You will be challenging your desires not to go back and associate with negative people who exercise at-risk behaviors, are in gangs, and affiliated with gang members. You must understand that other young people have failed in trying to meet these very same challenges that you now face. Many are dead, locked up, and some are even in mental institutions. You do not have to make those same mistakes. You

can meet your challenges head on and learn and grow from them.
Assignment:

Write out your outline of the challenges you will face in keeping yourself out of gangs, affiliated with gangs, and practicing at-risk behaviors.

Write out the changes that you have made so far and the changes that you will make in your future. Be very detailed.

You are now using a different mindset to challenge yourselves to be successful in life.

What have you learned from your past? What are some of the things you need to work on to change your lives?

What other challenges do you expect to meet in your life in the near future?

Will you choose to listen to and learn from others?

How will you handle negative friends and family?

What makes you important to the world, society, and your community? Be very detailed. Write at least two pages.

Education and Transformation

Moving the Mountain

Directions:

Participants have now arrived at the stage in Groomed for Success where they will conduct an intense profile on self.
Self-Profile

Part 1

1. Picture
2. Name
3. Sex
4. Birth date
5. Residence
6. Height
7. Weight
8. Traits
9. Special Skills
10. Strengths
11. Weaknesses
12. Preferred traits of BF/GF
13. Favorite place to hang out
14. Favorite book/ author
15. Favorite movie/ TV show
16. Favorite music genre
17. Favorite band/ musician
18. Favorite actor/ actress
19. Most wanted thing now
20. First crush
21. Favorite game

Part 2

Ideal Vision for your Life:

You will clarify your wildest dreams, deepest needs, and unspoken desires.

Thriving Relationships:

You will clarify the primary people who empower you in your personal and professional life.

Higher Purpose:

You will clarify what your soul desires you to manifest to thrive and fulfill your destiny.

True Self Identity:

You will clarify your true essence, soul virtues, and personal truths independent from others' expectations or images

Spiritual Well Being:

You will clarify your ideals, highest values, and spiritual/religious truths that guide and inspire you.

Mental Well Being:
You will clarify your thoughts, beliefs, attitudes regarding: Money, Love, Power, World, Health, Spirit, and any theme you choose.

Emotional Well Being:

You will clarify your ability to access and express feelings in a healthy way, ranging from anxiety, fear, sadness, confusion, anger, and frustration to acceptance, peace, love, joy, gratitude, and etc.

Physical Well Being:

You will clarify your concerns with diet, exercise, sexuality, home life, finances, and etc.

Part 3

Write three to five sentences for each of the words below to describe yourself.

Values	Priorities	Interests	Skills	Talents	Roles
Life Style	Needs	Concerns	Abilities	Achievements	
Self Concept	Personalities	Motivations	Preferred Environment		

Part 4

Considering the fact that earlier in your program you wrote out your pros and cons list, you will now revisit or if you choose to, write out another pros and cons list. This time your pros and cons list should be much different than your previous list.

You have the ability within yourself to do whatever it is that you put your mind to. You can and will accomplish great things in your life. Your thoughts are energy and nothing that you think will ever come back to you void or empty. With all of your full measures and the positive energy that you put behind your actions, you will succeed in ways you have never even dreamed about. With this in mind, you are continually grooming yourself for success every day, mentally, emotionally, spiritually, and physically. The sky is the limit for you!

This energy that you have in you should always be directed in a positive manner, no matter what. If at any time you find yourself in a situation where you cannot exert your energy in a positive and healthy manner, then you must have a backup plan. You can always exit and if exiting is not an option, then you can choose to be silent. You must realize that you are exiting or silencing yourself for your own safety. You are doing what is in the best interest of yourself. Remember, you have made a solid commitment to yourself to always keep yourself safe from all hurt, harm, and danger.

An educated mind can accomplish great things. You can read about scientists and psychologists who have discovered how great your mind is and how powerful your thought process is. Knowing that you have a strong mind, will, and spirit is the developing characters that begin to shape your thinking and actions. Grooming yourself for success today will afford you to live the lifestyle that you choose to live.

There will be times in your life when you do all the right things and make all the right moves and things will still turn out wrong. You cannot afford to become discouraged. You need to know that that is a part of life and growing up. Things do not always turn out the way you may want them to, but you press on. You handle the things that you can handle at that time. You have to understand that in life there are ups and downs and it is how you choose to handle those ups and downs that will give you your success. You are being restored and relearning to use your mind and power of choice in your own best interest. Always keep your whole person positive and healthy.

You are being groomed as strong, intelligent, brave, conscientious, honest, and caring young men and women. You will look after yourselves and each other with honesty and respect. You will take great pride and interest in your life today. You are developing your character right now. You have the heart of a warrior and you are equipped to fight any spiritual, physical, emotional, and mental battle that you may encounter in your everyday life. Always see the positive and focus on that. Never let the negative take root. Dismiss it right away and replace it with the positive energy that you possess. You have the necessary tools to be loyal and true to yourself and one another. You have the ability to move mountains!

You will now look over and input information into your (RTS) Roadmap to Success. You will start out with your anticipation of your last thirty days in the program. What will that consist of? Will you enroll in school, college, or military? Will you find a church home? What relationships will you seek out? Personal and Professional. What relationships will you avoid and how will you avoid them? What organizations will you join? What will you do for the community? Will you volunteer? Will you set practical goals? What kind of activities will you participate in and when? What will be your daily routine? What will you do for physical activity? Do you have short and long term goals and the way you plan to accomplish them written out in detail?

These are some of the questions you should be able to answer in writing your RTS. Your roadmap should be very detailed and there is an example to follow. (Note: Your roadmap will be different from every one's else's because no two people are the same). It is required that you write out a very detailed outline from your POP and then transfer your information from your POP onto your RTS. This RTS that you are creating is a document that you will refer to a lot for the next two years so you need to be clear about what you want and how you will attain the things that you want out of life, step by step.

Example of a (RTS) Roadmap to Success:

During the last thirty days of program: Job seeking starting at day one, attends school, go to the YMCA and work out, and visit a museum. By the time the last week arrives for me to leave the program, I want to be in full-time school and have a steady church family or other religious institution. I have a network of family and friends but that will grow over time. I want to volunteer at one of the local churches or teen centers. I will look for work and attempt to get a part time job. I will begin an exercise routine. I will be up at 8:00 each morning and attend a teen group each day.

30 days out of program: Housing secured on day one, attend school on day two, go to a meeting, attend a teen group each day, secure employment, visit churches or other religious institutions, start a club or join a club. Monitor a child, go help one of the elders from your church or from your committee.

60 days: Getting more comfortable with yourself and your environment, practicing kindness and learning how to be your brother's and sister's keeper in my committee and abroad.

90 days: Seeing and embracing your new self, feeling good about your change, ready to test for your GED, having positive interactions, having positive friends and family in your life. Start to set goals and strengthen yourself for the challenges you will be facing.

120 days: After 120 days, you should be becoming well rounded with a healthy spirit and a reasonable mental disposition.

You will continue to map out your routine until you reach your two year point in thirty day increments.

Be very detailed with yourself and stick to your routine and schedule.

You are Shining Stars: A Message to You All

You are bright and brilliant young people. You are shining stars. Some of you have lived a life of anger, pain, and disappointments in very stressful situations and environments. You have not been given a fair chance to be who you are capable of being. You have been placed in a condition which makes it extremely hard to focus on being a successful teen, and in some cases, even being a child. Living in such situations as those affords you no knowledge of self.

Groomed for Success has assisted you out of your previous mindsets and has put you on the path to true life success. We have assisted you mentally, physically, emotionally, and spiritually with the best education that we offer and that is the discovery of the knowledge of self. You have been dressed for your future success. You are now capable of rising above your situation and have the needed skills and resources to assist you in all areas of your life. Now it is your courage, tenacity, and growth that will take away your issues of low self-esteem, discouragements, anger, and at-risk conduct. You have brought forth the winner in you.

Remember your 'swag and shine' doesn't come from money, clothing brands, and relationships, but from you having the knowledge of self. You must remember this always, "To Thy Own

Self Be True". This is where your real swag and shine comes from, within you.

Questions:

Do you think that youth in some cities in the disenfranchised communities have had a fair chance to be who they want to be? If yes or no explain in detail.

What about you has changed since you began this program? How do you feel about those changes?

Do you feel this program has helped you? How? Explain in detail.

If not, what can Groomed for Success do to help you?

Part 5

Using Parts 1 through 4 and based on the information discovered in each part, write out a paper relating to yourself and the world, "Who Are You?"

What Do You Do When Stopped by Law Enforcement, Part 2?

Directions:

We suggest that an interaction workshop be conducted at the end of each phase. We also suggest that participants visit police stations to see law enforcement at work.

Participants should see Law Enforcement at work and interact with them. The young person's interaction with law enforcements will take the mis-presentation out of their minds and allow them to see these Law Enforcement officers as men and women having a job to do, as everyone else, who are employed to pay bills and make a living for self.

At the end of Phase 2, participants will express their feelings about the men and women in uniform. They will also express why they want to be a Law Enforcer or why they don't want to be a Law Enforcer.

Lesson 3

Groomed For Success

Groomed for Success

Turning Boys into Men/ Girls into Ladies

Directions:

In this section, the participant will examine what encompasses being a man or a woman. They will look at fatherhood and motherhood, morals, character, trust, and dependability and the overall life skill necessary to succeed in a proper manner.

Turning Boys/Girls Into Men and Women:

In this part of the program, this is very critical and important to the lives of our young people and to the one parent homes in America. To turn boys and girls into good parents and strong mentally, spiritually, and healthy men and women. This means to teach them how to think as a young man or a young woman. There are no real instructions to manhood and womanhood, but we as (tillers) teachers of minds must understand the mindset we are dealing with today.

We must first take out of the young males and females what was put in them. We can replace the independence of parenthood back into the spirits of these young ones by taking the foolish hearts out and putting a heart of a real man and a real woman into the youth today. What was handed down to our young people from generation to generation was in some cases unaware recklessness.

There are many ways to address these mindsets our youth have today and Groomed for Success is a remedy that our participants have been given. We first want our youth to understand they are their brother's and sister's keeper and they are that village which it takes to raise one child.

Questions:

What are some of the main points you need to look at?

How can you turn yourself into a peaceful, loving young man and woman and be your brothers' and sisters' keeper?

How can you be the man and woman at home and be a positive road model for your little brothers and sisters at home and in the neighborhoods?

Groomed for Success

Bridging the Gap

Directions:

Participants will start to bridge the gap. They will mend their broken relationships with family and society.

Bridging the Gap:

There are many circumstances in life that mandate a gap to be bridged. In this program, we will route this subject via repairing broken hearts, broken relationships, and many things young people have done in their community that was not correct. It will reestablish him/her with a positive attitude and a fresh approach in the participant's community. How many times have "you" told your loved ones you were sorry, and that you will not do it again, and you did it again and again?

To mend broken relationships means you have to change from your previous state of mind and negative activities. When you break a bond and the trust between you, your loved ones, or friends, they will not trust you until you earn that trust back. In some cases, it could take a lot of time, months and maybe years to gain their complete trust in you again. We all owe or have owed apologies to someone. It's time and it is your duty to humble yourself to those loved ones and friends with an apology.

Questions:

If you trust someone and they break the bond and trust of friendship, what do you think it would take for you to gain their trust back?

Do you think you have changed while in this program?

Are you ready to apologize to your loved ones and friends?

What does being humble mean to you?

What does bridging the gap means to you?

Your assignment is to write out a letter to loved ones and or friends to apology for your mistakes.

If you like, you can mention the things you have done and why you did them.

Start your letter of apology.

Society

Society is humanity, mankind, and or civilization. This is where we all live together in peace, in love, in wars, violence, and even stress and oppression, some of us but we all got to live together on this earth in one way or the other. The same goes for our neighborhoods and different committees where all the American people reside in. You must not take advantage of the freedom and the liberty we, as Americans, are given in society to be free and to embrace one another with love, peace, and hope. We know sometimes fairness and justice lacks and occasionally is absent because we don't live in a perfect world but for the most part, we are free to be who we want to be and do what is right toward one another in our society. We are in a position to love self and others and do what's right to one another and live in peace, but this is your choice.

Questions:
If you were to apologize to society what would you say?
Please write a letter apologizing to society for what you have done.
What is humanity?
If society has wronged you, what are their faults?
What would you tell the American people if you could stand before them and speak?
What do you owe to society?
What does society owe you as a citizen of America?
Please write your statement in detail.

Groomed for Success

Linking of the Souls and Spirits, Part 2

Directions:

Participants will complete their second and final self-evaluation. They will have a clear and concise understanding of who they are and how they will achieve their life goals.

The Linking of the Souls:

    Spirits and souls adhere to one another. This is found especially in family members and very close friends. This union that come from and through psychic experiences, such as suffering, emotions, and or some kind of traumatic experiences, loved ones can feel for others. These feelings bring attributes of sorrows and despairs. We are given souls and spirits as torchbearers. We shared experiences of those souls and spirits presents and others past lives. Some spirits have been distorted and disturbed and some people's spirits is handed down to relive other people's events. Being linked to other's positive spirits and souls can come from healthy spirits and positive thoughts. Be followers of good and do well in others life.

    We are our brothers' and sisters' keeper.

Groomed for Success

Expression of Your Higher Self

Directions:

Participants, at the end óf the promgram, will present an expression of their inner or higherself. This should be in the form of a public presentation. Participants will also recount what they have learned in the program and will have a written and detailed roadmap.

This topic, The Inner or Higher Self, can be expressed in a letter, a R&B song the participant has written, a postive rap song, or a poem. After the participant's brief presentation of their higher self, they will have written out a roadmap where their higher-self has them so far in this program, what they have learned thus far, and who they will become in the near future in detail.

In the beginning of this assignment, expressing participant's inner or higher self, there will be no profanity language, no "N" words, "B" words, gangster rap, and no omissions (slip-ups).

Example:

The Expression of Your Inner/ Higher Self:

We must express kindness and love to one another regardless of race, nationality, or ethnic group. Regardless of others' religion, spirituality, financial status, faults, and others' defeats, we must share positive information and give others positive tools to work with to meet their challenges in their lives. To strengthen one another means to go that extra mile and go back and lend a helping hand to those who are weakened and are in need of help.

If there is a spiritual existence when we leave this earth (death), I feel the only way I would be able to be there or go to that place is that I must help my brothers and sisters first to reside in their higher-self (best conduct) here and now, then I can peacefully and happily, without any guilt, say I have done my best toward others. While continually sharing my portions of life with others who need me and while sharing with others, I'll tell those who I'm sharing with to go out there with their portions and share with those who are lacking the expression of their higher self in their lives.

The message is this, we must look after one another because we are our brothers' and sisters' keeper and protector and this is what the higher consciousness relays to us. This message will come to you one day from your higher selves. Be the best you can be now.

Roadmap for Success (RFS) and Plan of Production (POP) is mandatory at the end of Phase 3 to have completed and ready for presentation.

Bibliography

[i] Wikipedia.com
[ii] Wikipedia.com
[iii] Wikipedia.com
[iv] Wikipedia.com
[v] Wikipedia.com
[vi] Wikipedia.com
[vii] http://usgovinfo.about.com/cs/mirandarights/a/miranda_2.htm
[viii] I Blame You, You and You: The Lost and Found Kids, Johnny Richey, Author House, 2012.
[ix] http://www.marcandangel.com/2013/11/17/10-harsh-realities-that-help-you-grow/
[x] http://en.wikipedia.org/wiki/Reality
[xi] http://www.sciencedaily.com/articles/s/sexually_transmitted_disease.htm
[xii] http://teens.drugabuse.gov/
[xiii] http://en.wikipedia.org/wiki/Peer_pressure
[xiv] http://en.wikipedia.org/wiki/Bullying
[xv] http://en.wikipedia.org/wiki/Gang
[xvi] http://en.wikipedia.org/wiki/Gangs_in_the_United_States
[xvii] http://gangresearch.net/Archives/UIC/Courses/history/beforethrash.html

www.ingramcontent.com/pod-product-compliance
Lightning Source LLC
LaVergne TN
LVHW040151080526
838202LV00042B/3110